rockschool®

Ukulele Debut

Performance pieces, technical exercises, supporting tests and in-depth guidance for Rockschool assessments

All accompanying and supporting audio can be downloaded from: *www.rslawards.com/downloads*

Input the following code when prompted: **WW8V969FCX**

For more information, turn to page 5

www.rslawards.com

Acknowledgements

Published by RSL Awards Ltd. © 2020
Catalogue Number: RSK200125US
ISBN: 978-1-78936-174-2
Initial US Release | Errata details can be found at *www.rslawards.com/errata*

SYLLABUS
Syllabus designed and written by Jono Harrison
Syllabus Director: Tim Bennett-Hart
Syllabus Consultants: Ashley Hards and Samantha Muir
Hit Tune arrangements by Ashley Hards, Giorgio Serci, Jono Harrison, Calum Harrison & Nat Martin
Supporting Tests written by Jono Harrison and Ashley Hards

PUBLISHING
Proof reading of arrangements by Jono Harrison, Ashley Hards & Calum Harrison
Music engraving, book layout and cover updates by Simon Troup and Jennie Troup of Digital Music Art
Fact files written and edited by Abbie Thomas
Proof reading and copy editing by Jono Harrison, Calum Harrison & Rosie Howard
Cover design by Philip Millard of Rather Nice Design
Cover photograph: © Olga Yatsenko (Shutterstock)

AUDIO
Produced by Jono Harrison
Mixed by Ian Caple & Jono Harrison
Engineered by Jono Harrison, Rory Harvey, Pete Riley, Giorgio Serci and Nat Martin
Supporting Tests recorded by Jono Harrison & Andy Robertson

MUSICIANS
Ukulele: Giorgio Serci, Samantha Muir, Nat Martin, Jono Harrison, Rory Harvey & Calum Harrison
Piano and Keyboards: Jono Harrison & Rory Harvey
Drums & Percussion: Pete Riley
Bass & Synth Bass: Rory Harvey
Guitars: Rory Harvey & Jono Harrison
Lead and Backing Vocals: Nick Shirm, Glen Harvey & Katy Virgoe
Additional Programming: Rory Harvey & Jono Harrison

EXECUTIVE PRODUCERS
John Simpson and Norton York

DISTRIBUTION
Exclusive distributors: Hal Leonard

CONTACTING ROCKSCHOOL
www.rslawards.com
Telephone: +44 (0)345 460 4747
Email: *info@rslawards.com*

Table of Contents

Introductions & Information

1 Title Page
2 Acknowledgements
3 Table of Contents
4 Welcome to Rockschool Ukulele Debut

Rockschool Level/Grade Pieces

7 'Demons' .... Imagine Dragons
11 'Knockin' On Heaven's Door' .... Bob Dylan
15 'Lean On Me' .... Bill Withers
19 'Marry You' .... Bruno Mars
25 'Rolling In The Deep' .... Adele
31 'Shake It Off' .... Taylor Swift

Technical Exercises

37 Group A | Scales
38 Group B | Arpeggios
39 Group C | Chord Voicings

Supporting Tests

40 Section 1 | Sight Reading
41 Section 1 | Improvisation & Interpretation
42 Section 2 | Ear Tests
43 Section 3 | General Musicianship Questions

About Rockschool Assessments

44 Entering Rockschool Assessments
44 Syllabus Guides
44 Performance and Technical Guidance
45 Marking Schemes

Additional Information

46 Ukulele Notation Explained
47 Copyright Information
48 Rockschool Digital Downloads

Welcome to Rockschool Ukulele Debut

Welcome to Rockschool's contemporary Ukulele syllabus 2020. This syllabus is designed to support ukulele players in their progression from Debut up to Level/Grade 8, through an engaging and rigorous pathway covering all the genres, stylistic elements, techniques and musical skills required for success as a contemporary ukulele player.

All elements required to participate in a Rockschool assessment can be found in the level/grade book. These are as follows:

Hit Tune Arrangements
The 2020 syllabus comprises six hit tune arrangements, meticulously researched and benchmarked to meet level/grade standards. The arrangements are devised so as to equip contemporary ukulele players with industry-relevant skills in any performance environment. These include:

- **All Levels/Grades**
  Four *'Session Style'* arrangements – focussing on developing skills required to perform in an ensemble environment, either in the studio or on stage. These arrangements cover accompaniment and lead playing skills.

- **Debut – Level/Grade 3**
  Two *'Duet'* arrangements – instrumental arrangements without a backing band, focussing on melody and accompaniment skills. The duet arrangements have a second part for teaching/ensemble purposes.

- **Levels/Grades 4–8**
  Two *'Solo'* arrangements, performed without backing track and arranged to test melodic and self-accompaniment skills.

Each Hit Tune arrangement is preceded by a Fact File, giving surrounding context to the piece and the original performers/recording artists.

Furthermore, you will find performance notes giving additional supportive context to get the most out of the pieces.

Technical Exercises
These are divided into groups at all levels/grades as outlined below:

- **Debut – Level/Grade 5** | Divided into *three* groups:
  Group A: Scales
  Group B: Arpeggios
  Group C: Chords

- **Levels/Grades 6–8** | Divided into *four* groups:
  Group A: Scales
  Group B: Arpeggios
  Group C: Chords
  Group D: Stylistic Studies

Supporting Tests

There are three sections in this part of the assessment. Please note that the sections contain differing elements depending on the level/grade:

Section 1

Sight Reading *or* **Improvisation & Interpretation** | *Debut – Level/Grade 5 only*
At Debut to Level/Grade 5, candidates can choose between the following:

- **Sight Reading** – a test of the musician's ability to read and perform previously unseen material
- **Improvisation & Interpretation** – a test of the musician's ability to develop previously unseen material in a stylistic way and perform improvised passages of melody. The book contains examples of both types of test. Equivalent 'unseen' examples will be provided for the assessment.

Quick Study Piece | *Levels/Grades 6–8 only*
At Levels/Grades 6–8, candidates must perform a previously unseen Quick Study Piece, combining the skills of the Sight Reading and Improvisation & Interpretation tests from earlier levels/grades.

Section 2

Ear Tests
Candidates must take all tests in this section. Ear tests feature at all levels/grades, but the elements differ as outlined below:

- **Melodic Recall** *and* **Rhythmic Recall** tests | *Debut – Level/Grade 3*
- **Melodic Recall** *and* **Harmonic Recall** tests | *Levels/Grades 4–8*

Section 3

General Musicianship Questions
Candidates must answer General Musicianship Questions (GMQ's) at all levels/grades, on one of their chosen pieces from the repertoire section. The nature of the questions differs depending on the level/grade. Please refer to the relevant section of the level/grade book for details.

Audio

All accompanying audio can be downloaded from RSL directly at *www.rslawards.com/downloads*. This includes backing tracks and full mixes of the level/grade pieces, examples of the technical exercises and supporting tests, and click tracks (where applicable). The audio files are supplied as MP3 format, and can be played using any compatible device.

You will need to input this code when prompted: **WW8V969FCX**

Note: If you have purchased a digital version of this book, you will be sent a link through which you can download the accompanying audio.

'Demons' | Imagine Dragons

Album: *Night Visions*
Label: Interscope/Kidinakorner
Genre: Pop/Rock
Chart Peak: 1 (US)

Written By: Ben Mckee, Adam Baachaoui, Dan Platzman, Dan Reynolds, Wayne Sermon, Alexander Grant, Josh Mosser
Produced By: Alex Da Kid

Background Info

'Demons' is a song recorded by American rock band Imagine Dragons. It was written by band members Dan Reynolds (vocals), Wayne Sermon (lead guitar), Ben McKee (bass), and Daniel Platzman (drums), and was produced by Alex da Kid. The song appears on their major-label debut extended play *Continued Silence* and also makes an appearance on their debut studio album *Night Visions* as the fourth track.

Night Visions was recorded between 2010 and 2012 and was primarily produced by the band themselves, as well as British hip-hop producer Alex da Kid and Brandon Darner, from the American indie rock group The Envy Corps.

The song has been a commercial success, becoming their second Top 10 single after their initial chart hit, 'Radioactive'. 'Demons' has sold over four million copies in the United States, and was the eighth most downloaded song in rock history as of 2015.

'Demons' managed an impressive 61 weeks on the US Hot 100 and won Imagine Dragons several awards, including the iHeart Radio Music Award for Alternative Rock Song of The Year in 2014. The song also achieved top ten positions in singles charts around the globe, including Canada, Belgium, Austria, Brazil and France.

The hallmark of Imagine Dragons' music is its ability to blur the lines between musical genres. Dan Reynolds cites Arcade Fire, Nirvana, Muse, The Beatles, Paul Simon, Coldplay, Harry Nilsson, and U2 as some of his and the band's artistic influences. In terms of success, Reynolds credits bands like Foster the People and Mumford & Sons for bringing alternative pop music to a new level of commercial success in recent years.

Performance Notes

This pop/rock song starts with a laid back feel but the intensity gradually builds through the different sections. The key centre is C major and your four chord progression remains constant throughout the song, but notice that your strumming pattern changes every eight measures.

The main challenge will be to move confidently between chords. You will be strumming on all four beats in the C section and you will need a fast and accurate change from one chord to the next. However, you must take particular care with the long chords in the A section because they must still be held for their four full beats. Listen carefully to the band so you can count the beat and stay in time.

Demons

Session Style

Imagine Dragons

Words and Music by Daniel Reynolds, Benjamin McKee, Daniel Sermon, Alexander Grant and Josh Mosser
Copyright © 2012 SONGS OF UNIVERSAL, INC., IMAGINE DRAGONS PUBLISHING, ALEXANDER GRANT and JMOSSER MUSIC
All Rights for IMAGINE DRAGONS PUBLISHING and ALEXANDER GRANT Controlled and Administered by SONGS OF UNIVERSAL, INC.
All Rights Reserved Used by Permission

'Knockin' On Heaven's Door' | Bob Dylan

Album: *Patt Garrett & Billy The Kid*
Label: Columbia
Genre: Folk/Gospel
Chart Peak: 12 (US)
Written By: Bob Dylan
Produced By: Gordon Carroll

Background Info

'Knockin' on Heaven's Door', written and performed by Bob Dylan, is taken from the soundtrack of the 1973 film *Pat Garrett and Billy the Kid*, Dylan's twelfth studio album. The song describes the final moments of a deputy sheriff; dying from a bullet wound as he assesses the world before his passing. Dylan also appeared in the film as the character 'Alias'. The soundtrack consists primarily of instrumental music inspired by the story depicted in Sam Peckinpah's western.

Released as a single, it reached number 12 on the US Billboard Hot 100 singles chart. The song's influence can be measured by the raft of other artists who have covered it (Eric Clapton, Guns N' Roses, Warren Zevon and Avril Lavigne to name a few) and is one of Dylan's most popular compositions.

Bob Dylan is an American singer-songwriter, artist and writer. He has been influential in popular music and culture for more than six decades. Much of his most celebrated work dates from the 1960s, with songs such as 'Blowin' in the Wind' and 'The Times They are a Changin'' that became anthems for the American Civil Rights Movement. Leaving behind his initial base in the American folk music revival, his six-minute single 'Like a Rolling Stone', recorded in 1965, enlarged the range of popular music and is seen as one of the most influential songs ever written.

Dylan's songs have defied existing pop music conventions and also appealed to the burgeoning counterculture that rose to prominence during the 1960s. Initially inspired by the performances of Little Richard and the song writing of Woody Guthrie, Robert Johnson, and Hank Williams, he has explored the traditions in American song. From folk, blues, and country to gospel and rock and roll, rockabilly to English, Scottish, and Irish folk music, even embracing jazz and the Great American Songbook.

Dylan's impressive list of accolades only confirms the staggering influence his work has had on the music industry as we know it today. Throughout his career he has won many prestigious awards, including an Academy Award, a Golden Globe and an incredible ten Grammy Awards. However, no award proves his worth as a writer more than his 2016 accomplishment of a Nobel Prize for literature.

Performance Notes

This classic song has a tempo of 65 bpm which will feel slow. The title suggests this song should sound sad and respectful, so it might seem a little confusing that the song is written in C major, because we know it normally sounds quite cheerful. However, an interesting feature of the chord progression is the F chord at the end which changes back to C as the progression starts again. This is very common in hymns, and maybe it adds to the respectful, reverent feel of the song.

The main challenge of the song will be the speed of the chord changes. The chords must ring before changing quickly to the next shape. Take care to play with a smooth even tone. The song must sound slow and stately even though it might feel like your fingers are moving quickly between the chords! Practise slowly at first to make sure your fingers are moving accurately between the chords, then you can gradually increase the tempo. There is a change in the strumming pattern for the chorus but make sure the chords still ring. The desired effect is to remain as smooth in the sound of the strumming as possible, whilst projecting cleanly and clearly.

'Lean On Me' | Bill Withers

Album: *Still Bill*
Label: Sussex
Genre: Soul

Chart Peak: 1 (US)
Written By: Bill Withers
Produced By: Bill Withers

Background Info

'Lean on Me' was written and recorded by American singer-songwriter Bill Withers. It was released in April 1972 as the first single from his second album, *Still Bill*. 'Lean on Me' was his first and only number one single and was ranked number 208 on *Rolling Stone's* list of 'The 500 Greatest Songs of All Time'.

Withers' childhood in the coal mining town of Slab Fork, West Virginia, was the inspiration for 'Lean on Me', which he wrote after he had moved to Los Angeles and found himself missing the strong community ethic of his hometown.

Wither's version is noted for its catchy bridge as well as the coda section, where the words "call me" are repeated a total of 14 times, before the song ends on a cadenza on the strings. Several radio stations have been known to fade out during the 6th repetition due to mainstream song length restrictions.

Bill Withers recorded several major hits, including 'Lean on Me', 'Ain't No Sunshine', 'Use Me', 'Just the Two of Us', 'Lovely Day', and 'Grandma's Hands'. He was nominated for seven Grammy Awards during his time as a performer and was awarded three of them.

Born with a stutter, Withers found it difficult to fit in socially during his early years. He enlisted with the United States Navy at the age of 18, served for nine years and having gotten over his stutter became interested in writing songs with renewed confidence. Leaving the Navy in 1965, he relocated to Los Angeles in 1967 to perform his compositions publicly.

Withers worked as an assembler for several different companies, while recording demo tapes with his own money and performing his early compositions in local nightclubs in the evenings. When he debuted with the song 'Ain't No Sunshine' he refused to resign from his job because he still felt he could not rely on the music industry for his future.

Performance Notes

Lean on me is a soul song performed at a slow, walking tempo of 76 bpm. The 4/4 time signature also tells us the music should be played with a steady, even feel. Your performance should be laid back but make sure you stay in time with the backing track. Think about how loud you should be playing to balance with the rest of the band and to get the right feel for the song. The song stays in C major which adds to the calm, peaceful feel.

You will be playing the melody during the verses. This is usually sung and it is really important to play it in a smooth 'singing' style by joining all your notes together *(legato)* and by playing with an even tone. Make sure you understand all the rhythms; especially the ties and dotted notes in the verses. The melody walks up and down the C major scale, so lots of practice with this scale will give you confidence in playing this piece.

You will be playing accompanying chords in the B section, and all of these chords come from the notes in the C major scale. There are rests in these measures, giving you plenty of time to change between most of the chords but look out for the faster changes in measures 12 and 16. The syncopation created by the dotted rhythms in these measures gives the song an exciting lift, so it is important to play this part carefully but with clear projection. Think about how loud you should play this section so it suits the song. Remember to mute the chords as the rhythm shows!

Lean On Me

Session Style

Bill Withers

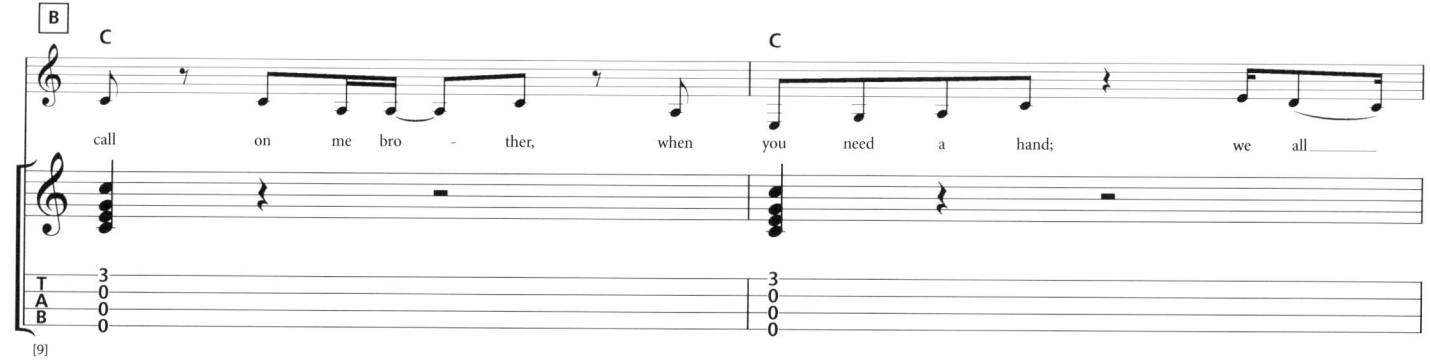
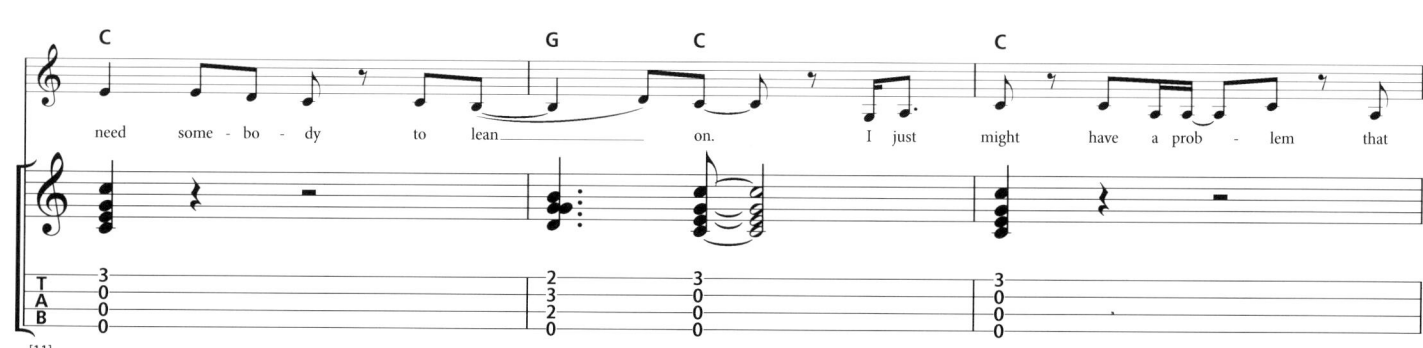

Words and Music by Bill Withers
Copyright © 1972 INTERIOR MUSIC CORP. Copyright Renewed
All Rights Controlled and Administered by SONGS OF UNIVERSAL, INC.
All Rights Reserved   Used by Permission

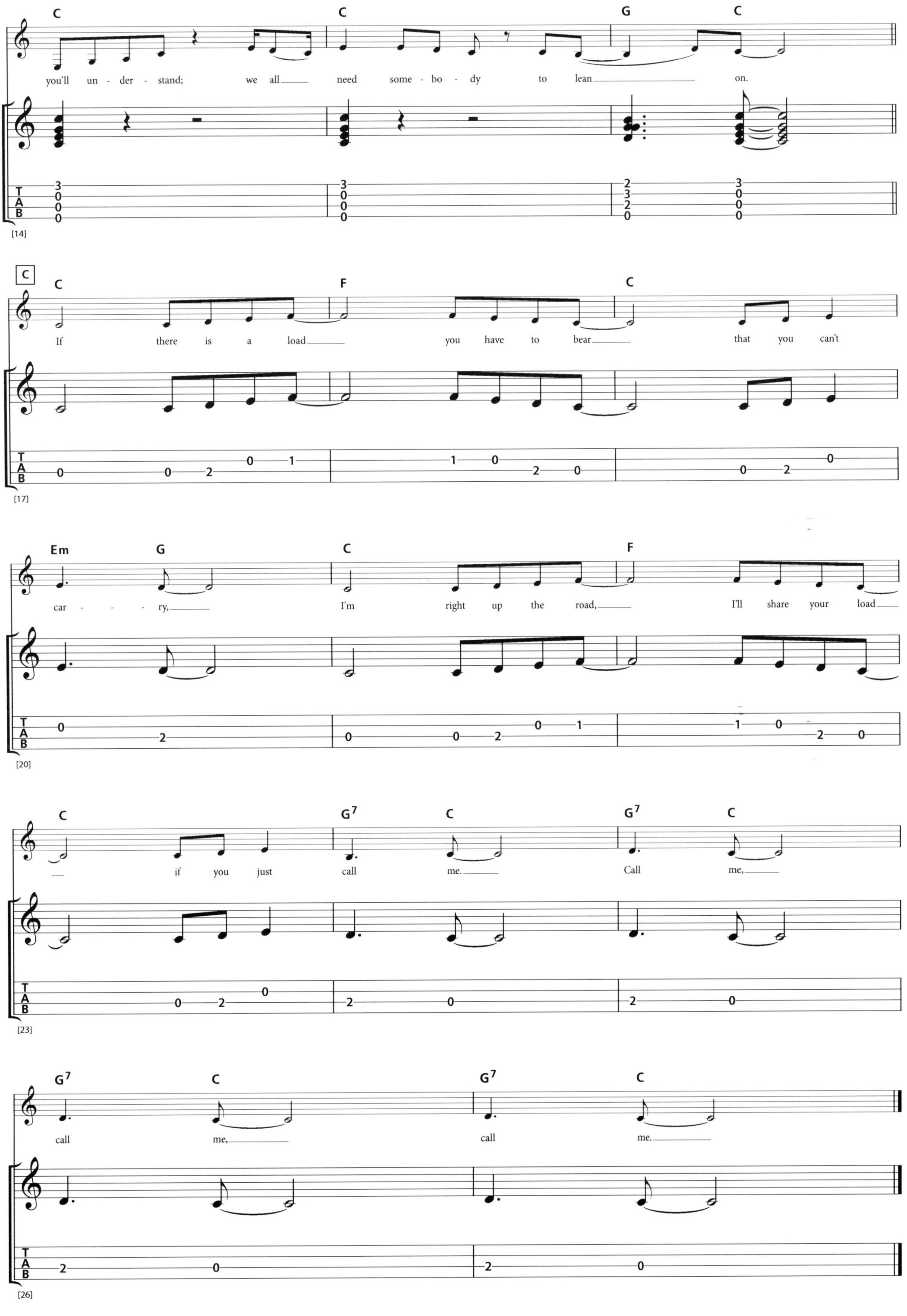
C C G C
you'll un - der - stand; we all need some - bo - dy to lean on.
[14]
C
C F C
If there is a load you have to bear that you can't
[17]
Em G C F
car - - - ry, I'm right up the road, I'll share your load
[20]
C G7 C G7 C
if you just call me. Call me,
[23]
G7 C G7 C
call me, call me.
[26]

'Marry You' | Bruno Mars

Album: *Doo-Wops & Hooligans*
Label: Elektra/Warner
Genre: Pop

Chart Peak: 85 (US)
Written By: Bruno Mars, Phillip Lawrence, Ari Levine
Produced By: The Smeezingtons

Background Info

'Marry You', by Hawaiian singer-songwriter Bruno Mars, featured on his debut studio album *Doo-Wops & Hooligans* (2010). The track was written and produced by The Smeezingtons (Mars, Philip Lawrence, and Ari Levine), a production team co-founded by Mars in 2009. 'Marry You' is a pop song strongly influenced by the close harmony doo-wop sound that became popular in the United States in the 1950s.

The song focuses on the theme of spontaneous marriage, which has led to it being frequently used as a popular choice for proposals. 'Marry You' received generally positive reviews from music critics, with some complimenting a production style that is reminiscent of 60s pop. The song has been covered a number of times, most notably by the cast of Glee.

'Marry You' debuted at number 91 on the Billboard Hot 100 in December 2010, with the song's reception being stronger outside of the United States. After the Glee performance of the track, 'Marry You' debuted at number 89 in Canada, whilst in the United Kingdom it peaked at number 11 and remained in the charts for 39 weeks.

Bruno Mars is a Hawaiian singer-songwriter, multi-instrumentalist, record producer, and choreographer. Born and raised by his musical family in Honolulu, Hawaii, Mars began making music at a young age and performed in various musical venues in his hometown throughout his childhood. He graduated from high school and moved to Los Angeles to pursue his musical career.

Since his debut, Mars has achieved five UK number 1 singles and two UK number one albums. His accolades so far include an impressive three Brit Awards, four Guinness World Records and eleven Grammy Awards.

Performance Notes

This pop song has a lively tempo, so be sure to count the down beats in each measure. It should sound happy and exciting, as shown by the key centre of the piece (C major). Think about the song title and make your playing fit the mood of the music.

The chord progression remains the same for the entire song but the main challenge will be to make the chord changes sound smooth. Hold the long chords at the start for eight beats (two measures) before a very quick change to the next chord. Count your beats carefully until you feel confident feeling when to change. Many pop songs are written in 4/4, so you will soon learn to feel music comfortably in this time signature. Your accompanist will be playing an exciting syncopated rhythm in the A section, so you must feel confident keeping the beat.

The B section has an interesting feel. You will be playing on beats two and four. Remember to mute the strings on beats one and three.

As this song is a duet arrangement, another challenge will be staying in time and keeping the pulse steady. Whether playing with another musician or the recording of the second part, it is important to focus on counting the four beats in every measure. Practice counting and tapping your foot to a metronome or drum loop at a slower tempo, and then slowly increase the tempo as you gain confidence.

Marry You

Candidate Part (Assessed)

Duet

Bruno Mars

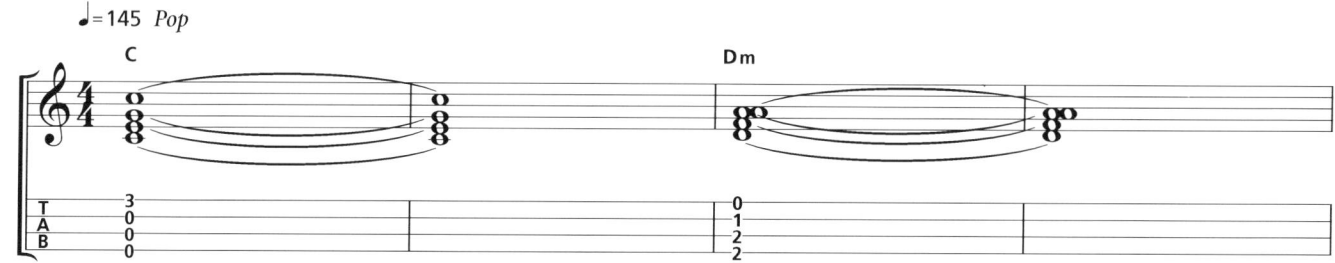

See note on welcome page about assessed and non-assessed ukulele parts

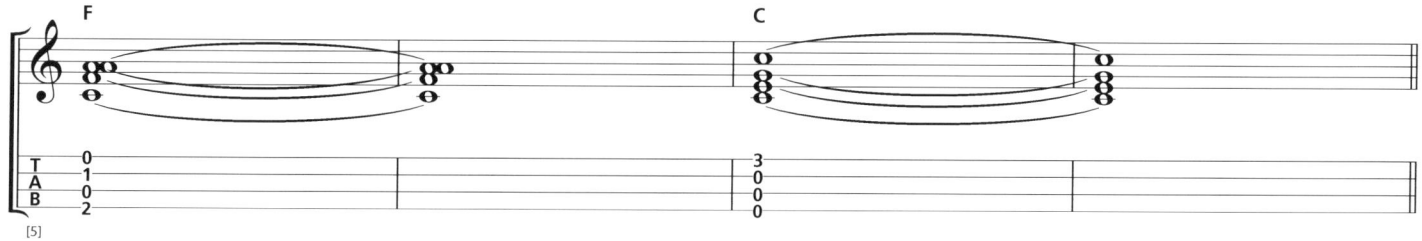

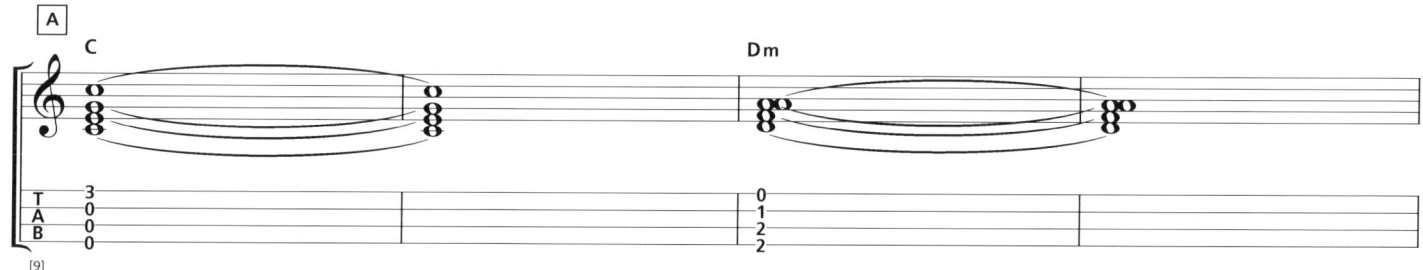

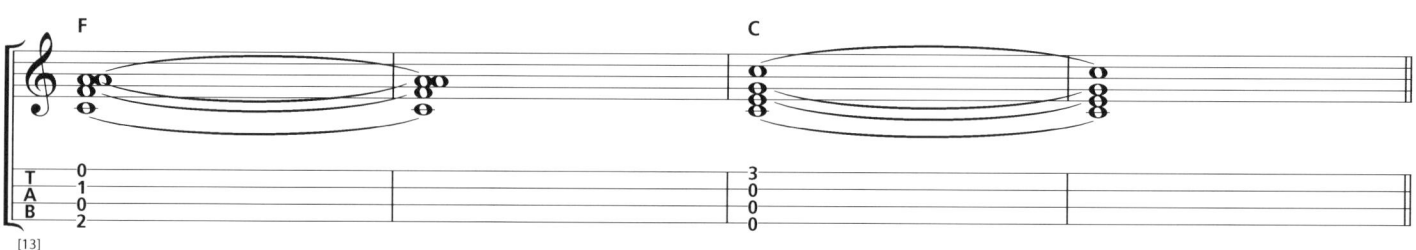

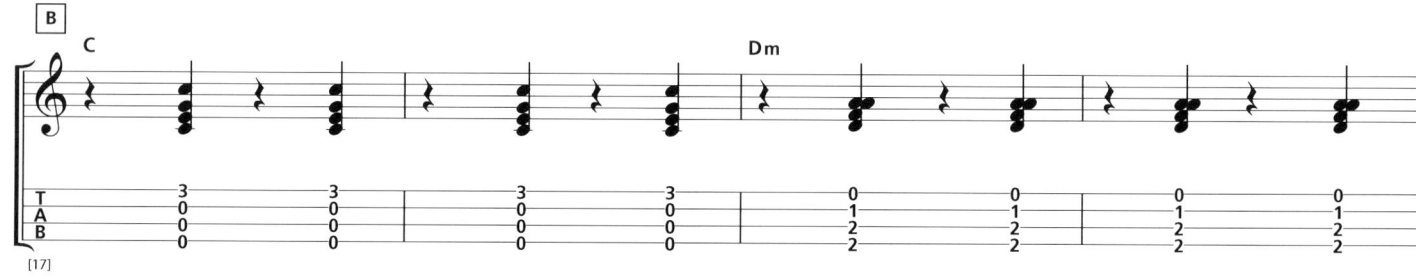

Words and Music by Bruno Mars, Ari Levine and Philip Lawrence
© 2010 BMG FIREFLY, BMG GOLD SONGS, MARSFORCE MUSIC, ROUND HILL SONGS, TOY PLANE MUSIC, NORTHSIDE INDEPENDENT MUSIC PUBLISHING, LLC, THOU ART THE HUNGER, ROC NATION MUSIC and MUSIC FAMAMANEM
All Rights for BMG FIREFLY, BMG GOLD SONGS, MARSFORCE MUSIC, ROUND HILL SONGS and TOY PLANE MUSIC Administered by BMG RIGHTS MANAGEMENT (US) LLC
All Rights for THOU ART THE HUNGER Administered by NORTHSIDE INDEPENDENT MUSIC PUBLISHING, LLC
All Rights for ROC NATION MUSIC and MUSIC FAMAMANEM Administered by WC MUSIC CORP.
All Rights Reserved   Used by Permission

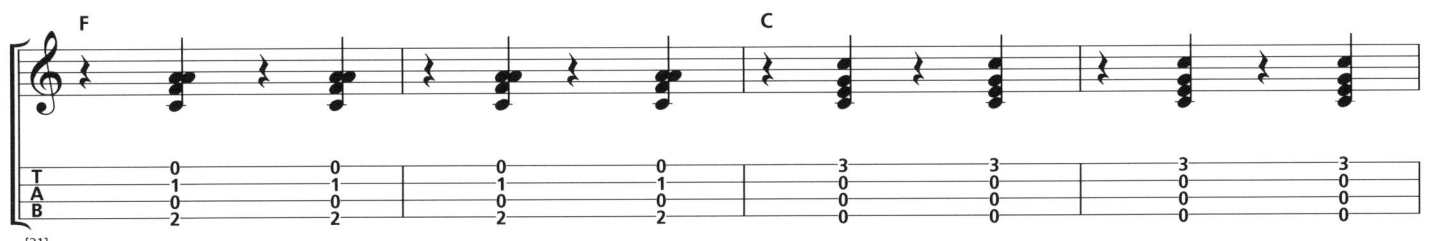
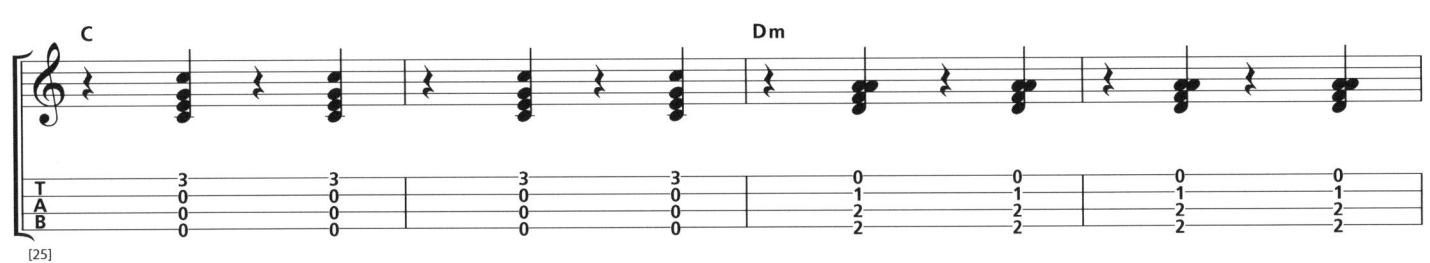
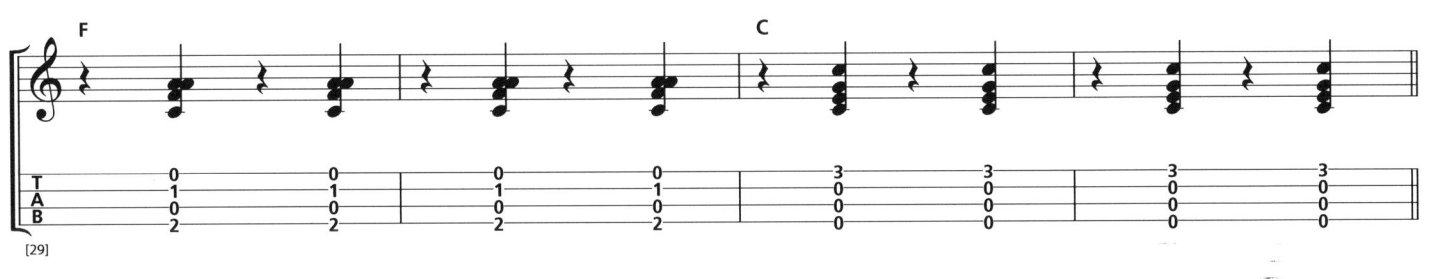
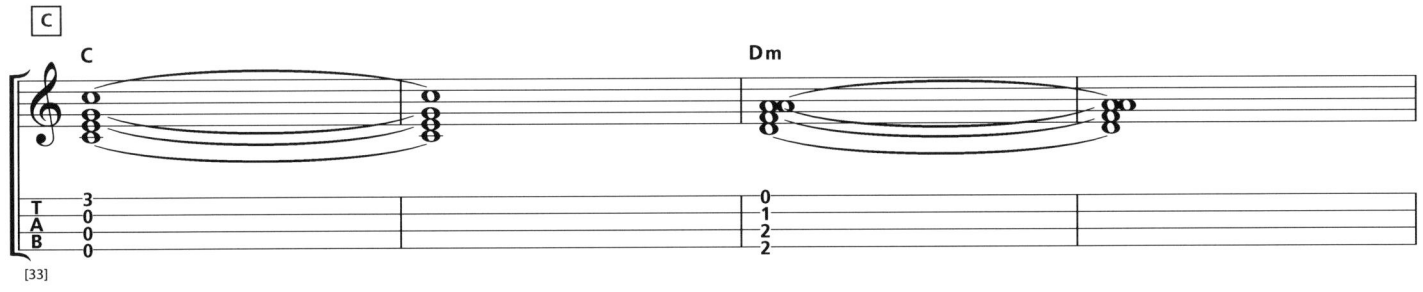
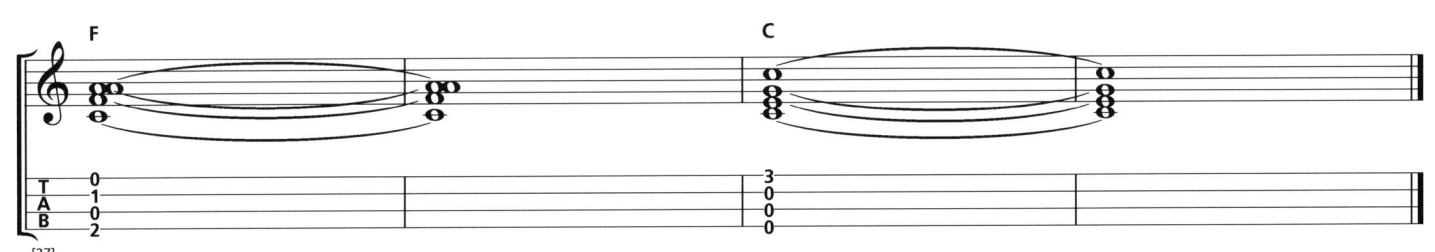

Marry You

Duet

Duet Part (Non-assessed)

Bruno Mars

See note on welcome page about assessed and non-assessed ukulele parts

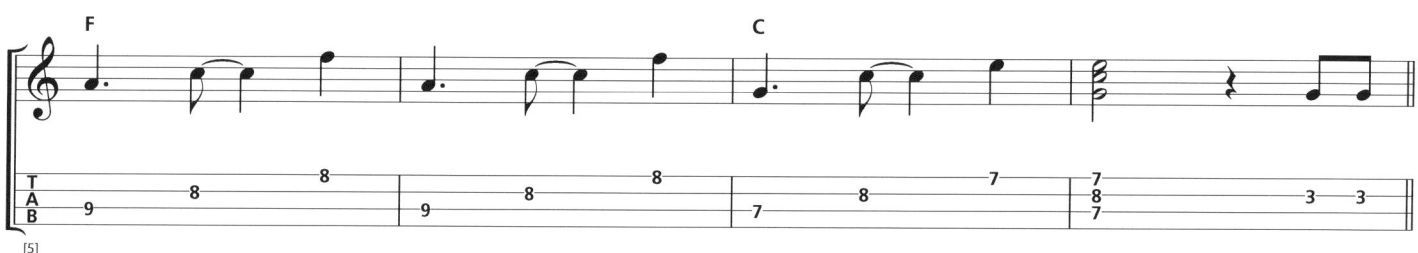

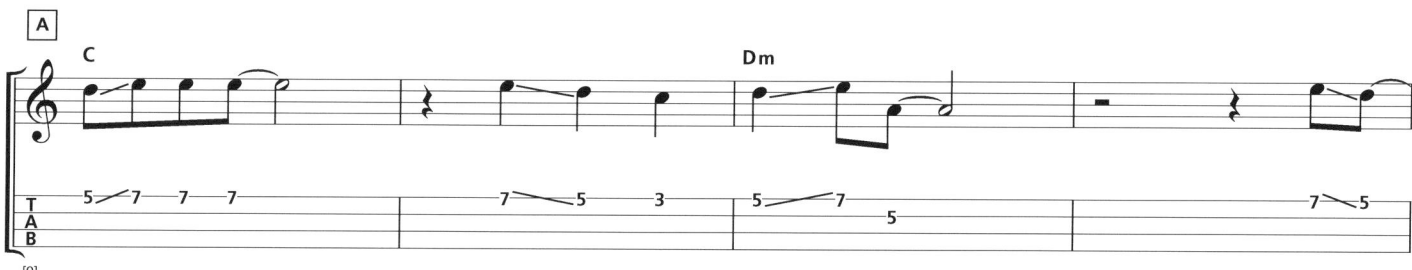

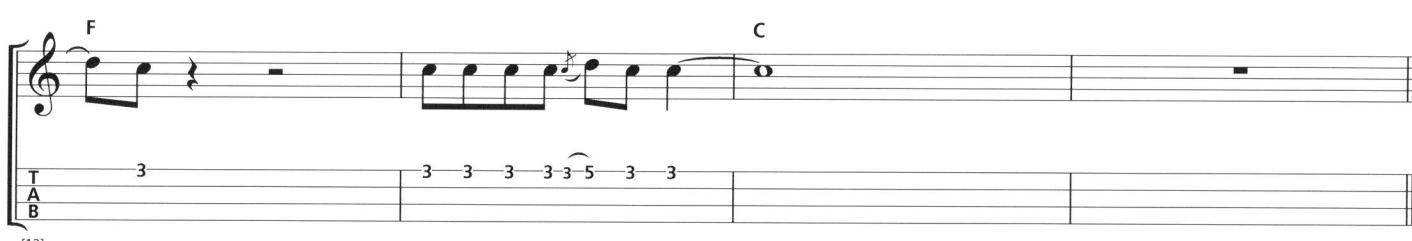

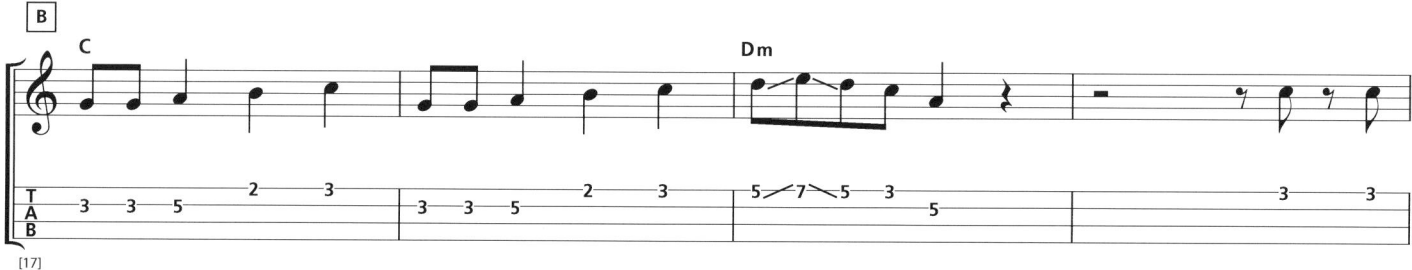

Words and Music by Bruno Mars, Ari Levine and Philip Lawrence
© 2010 BMG FIREFLY, BMG GOLD SONGS, MARSFORCE MUSIC, ROUND HILL SONGS, TOY PLANE MUSIC, NORTHSIDE INDEPENDENT MUSIC PUBLISHING, LLC, THOU ART THE HUNGER, ROC NATION MUSIC and MUSIC FAMAMANEM
All Rights for BMG FIREFLY, BMG GOLD SONGS, MARSFORCE MUSIC, ROUND HILL SONGS and TOY PLANE MUSIC Administered by BMG RIGHTS MANAGEMENT (US) LLC
All Rights for THOU ART THE HUNGER Administered by NORTHSIDE INDEPENDENT MUSIC PUBLISHING, LLC
All Rights for ROC NATION MUSIC and MUSIC FAMAMANEM Administered by WC MUSIC CORP.
All Rights Reserved Used by Permission

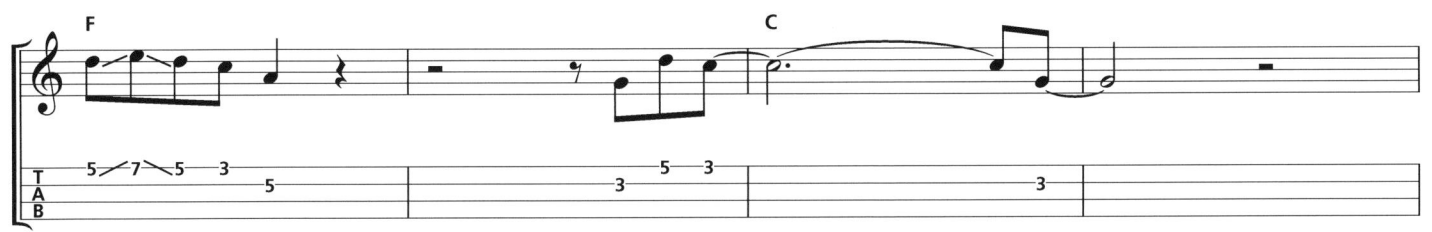
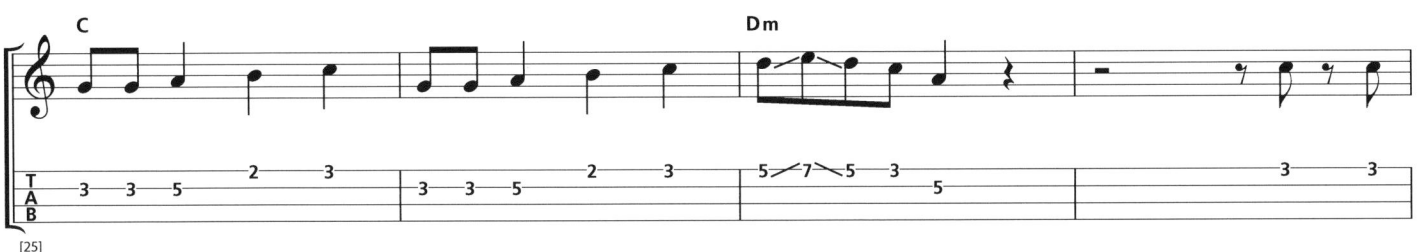
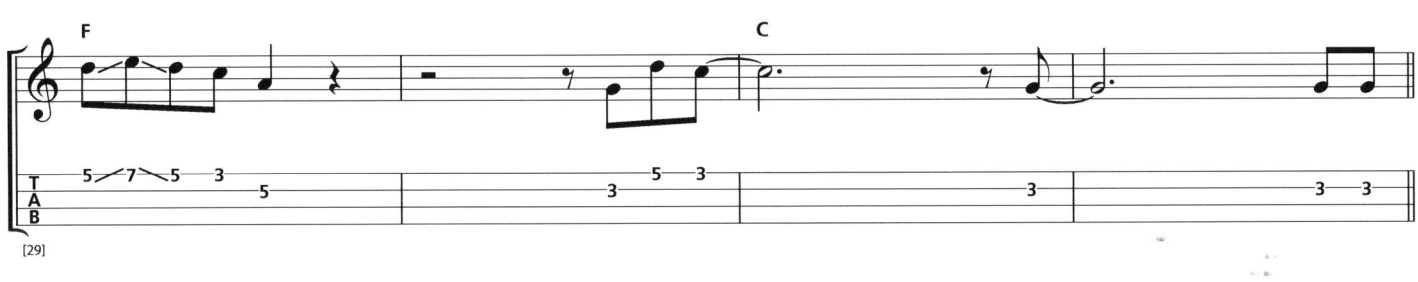
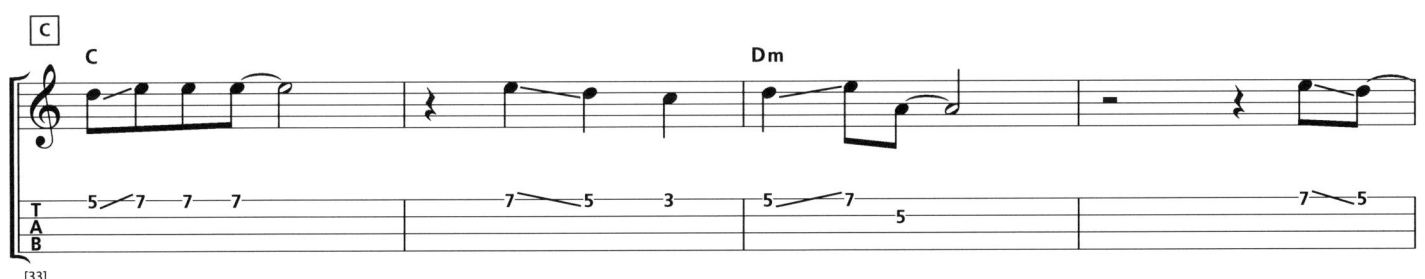
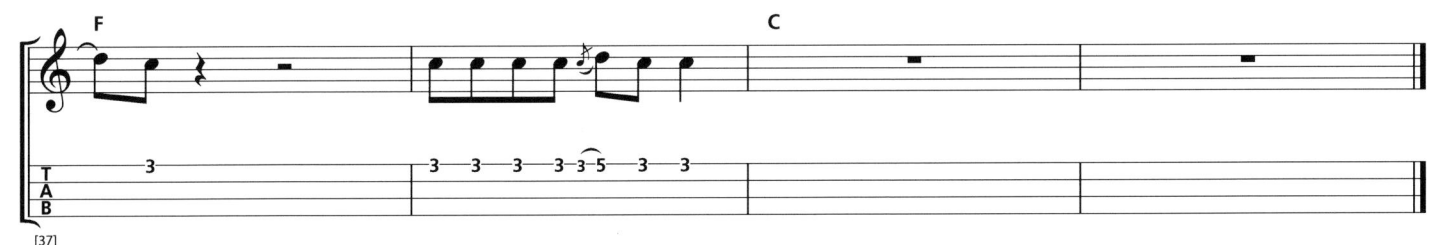

'Rolling In The Deep' | Adele

Album: *21*
Label: XL
Genre: Pop/Soul

Chart peak: 1 (US)
Written By: Adele Atkins, Paul Epworth
Produced By: Paul Epworth

Background Info

'Rolling In The Deep' was released as a single in November 2010 and became an international chart topper. The song appears on Adele's second album *21*. 'Rolling In The Deep' was met with critical and commercial acclaim and became a record breaking hit, spending 65 weeks on the US charts and selling over 20 million digital copies worldwide, making it the second best-selling digital single of all time. In the US 'Rolling In The Deep' sold over 7.5 million copies and became the biggest crossover hit of the past 25 years. The song also received three Grammy Awards, for Record Of The Year, Song Of The Year and Best Short Form Music Video. 'Rolling In The Deep' is the fourth song to top the Billboard Year-end Hot 100 singles chart and win Grammy Awards for Best Record and Best Song of the Year in the same year.

Adele wrote 'Rolling In The Deep' in collaboration with acclaimed producer Paul Epworth, who also played guitars and bass on the recording. The lyrics were inspired by the breakup of a relationship. Adele was told by someone she was showing weakness by not staying in the said relationship and wrote the lyrics as a reaction to that. Although Adele was initially reluctant about a writing partnership with Epworth, she gained increased confidence in her vocal ability and expressive qualities as a result of working with him.

Adele signed to XL after graduating from the BRIT School of Performing Arts and Technology. Her debut album *19* was a huge critical and commercial success on both sides of the Atlantic. Her second album, *21*, sold over 31 million copies worldwide. She followed the success of *21* with the song 'Skyfall', recorded for the James Bond film of the same name, winning an Oscar, a Grammy Award and a Golden Globe Award and topping the charts. Adele's third album, *25*, recorded after a three year hiatus, was also a huge success, winning five Grammy Awards and selling millions worldwide. Her 2016-17 world tour broke attendance records. Adele has sold over 100 million records and is one of today's best-selling music artists.

Adele is praised for the quality of her voice and phrasing and the emotive way in which she conveys lyrics, always drawing attention to the song.

Performance Notes

This duet arrangement gives you the opportunity to play the melodic line and the rhythmic accompaniment. The song is played at a moderate tempo but the minor key and relentless rhythmic drive makes it sound intense and dark. Make the melody clear and precise to match the smouldering feel of the song.

It is important to be confident with the rhythms through the verse. The accompanying ukulele does not always change chords where you would expect so it is important to play your phrases carefully. The song should feel dark and moody at the start to match the tone of the lyrics.

A short repetitive phrase makes an interesting feature in the bridge. Look how the same pattern is used three times in a row between measures 5 and 8, then again between 9 and 12. The repetition creates tension as the song builds towards the chorus.

You will be playing the accompaniment during the chorus so it is important to support the other ukulele player by maintaining a steady pulse. Play with a strong, clear tone but always listen to make sure you are not drowning out the melody.

Rolling In The Deep

Duet

Candidate Part (Assessed)

Adele

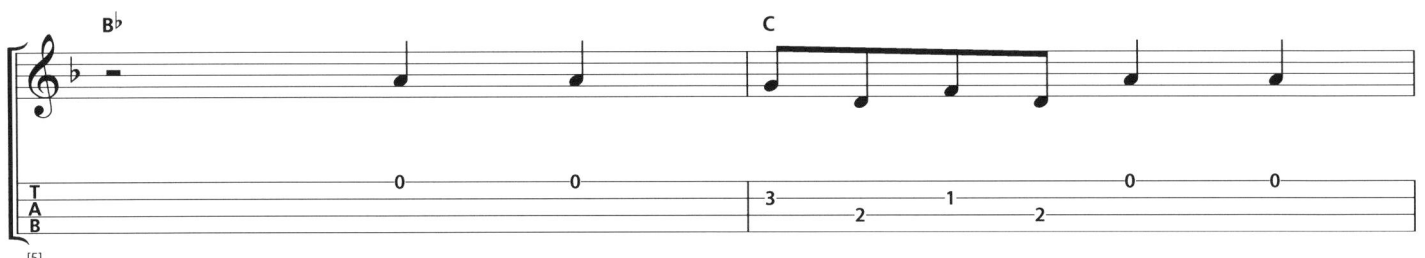
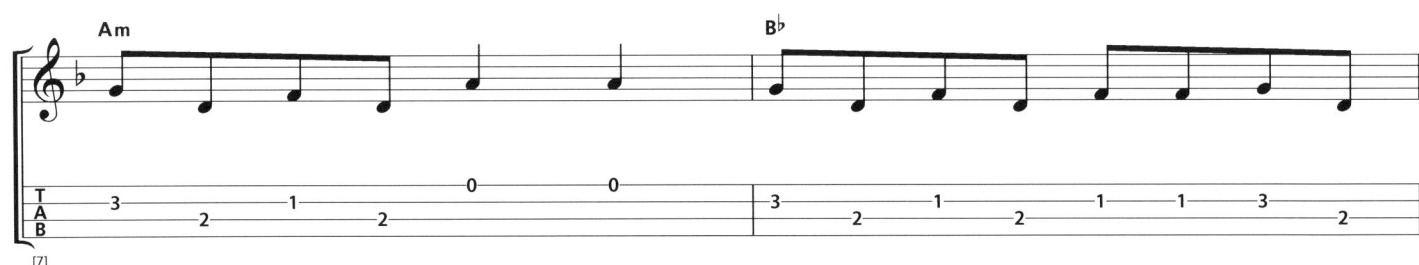
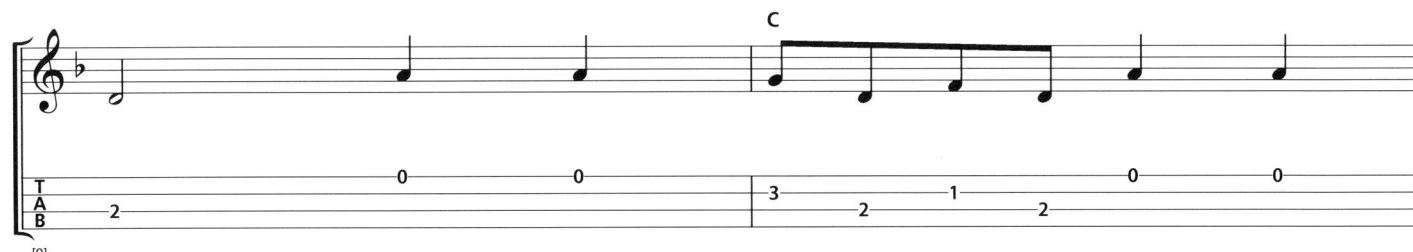

Words and Music by Adele Adkins and Paul Epworth
Copyright © 2010, 2011 MELTED STONE PUBLISHING LTD. and EMI MUSIC PUBLISHING LTD.
All Rights for MELTED STONE PUBLISHING LTD. in the U.S. and Canada Controlled and Administered by UNIVERSAL - SONGS OF POLYGRAM INTERNATIONAL, INC.
All Rights for EMI MUSIC PUBLISHING LTD. Administered by SONY/ATV MUSIC PUBLISHING LLC, 424 Church Street, Suite 1200, Nashville, TN 37219
All Rights Reserved   Used by Permission

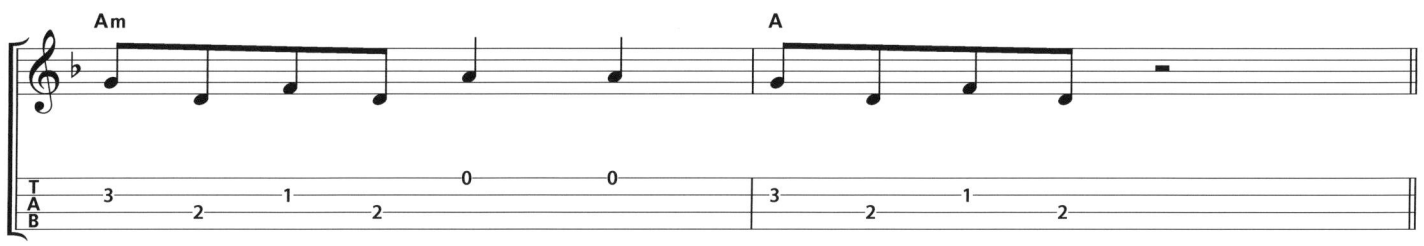
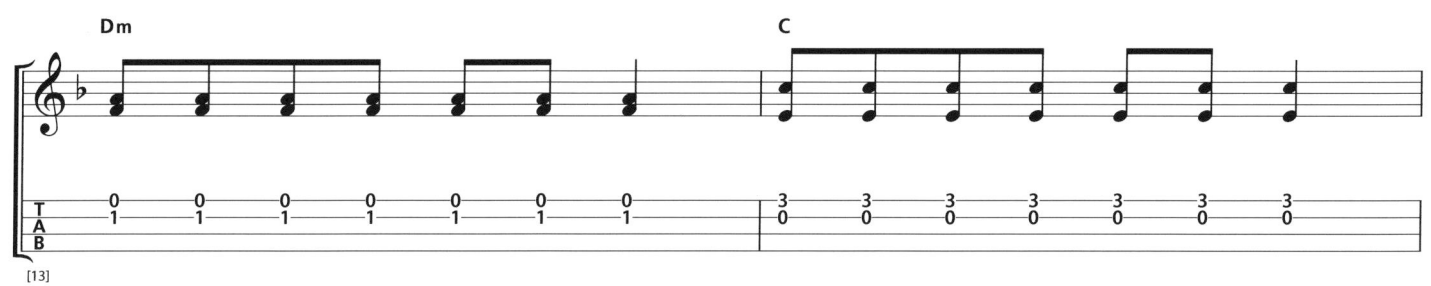

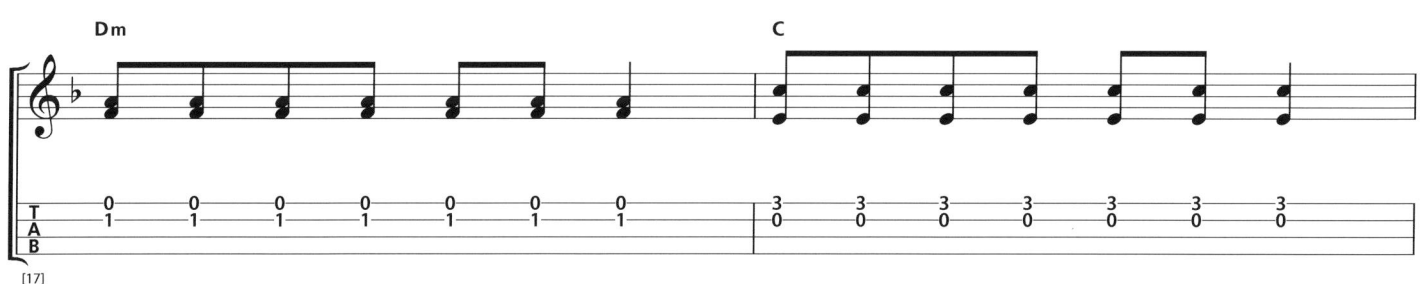
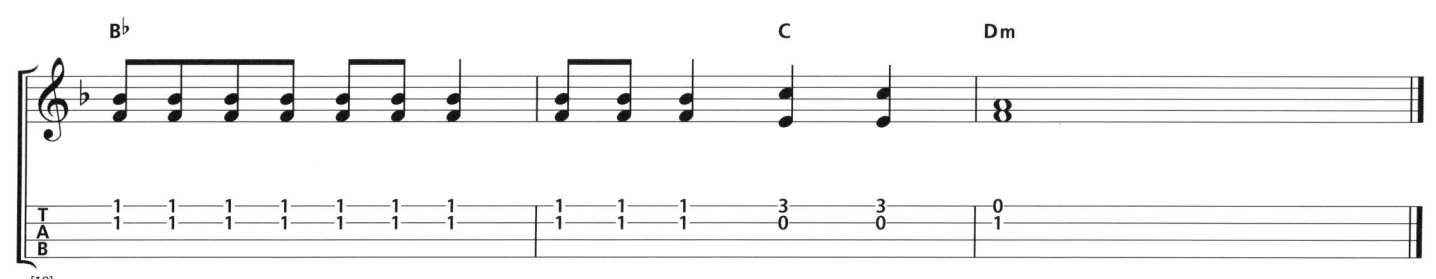

Rolling In The Deep

Duet

Duet Part (Non-assessed)

Adele

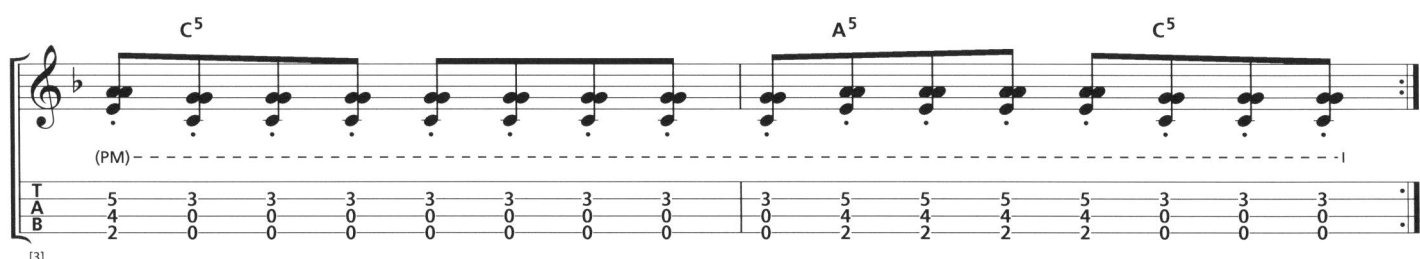
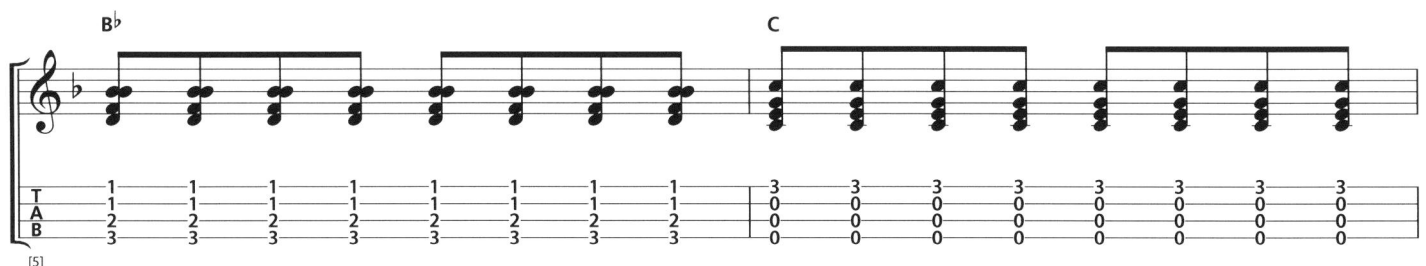
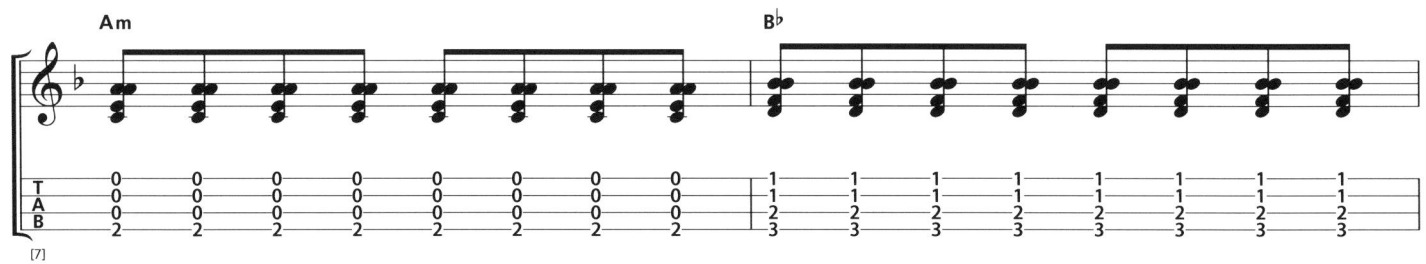
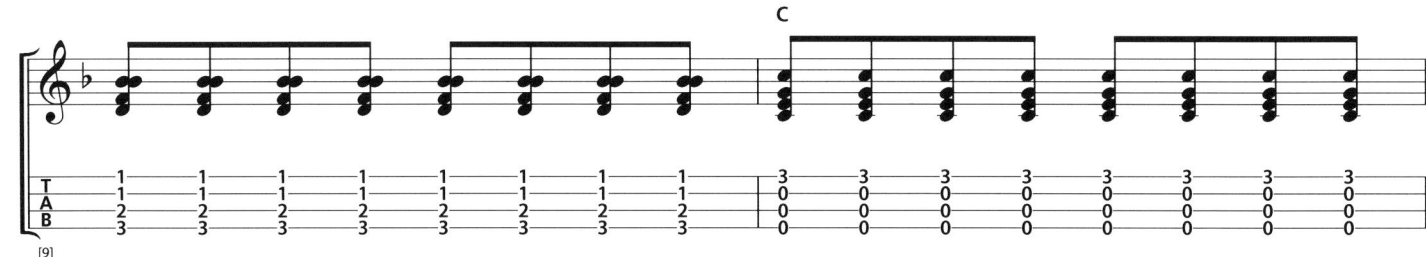

Words and Music by Adele Adkins and Paul Epworth
Copyright © 2010, 2011 MELTED STONE PUBLISHING LTD. and EMI MUSIC PUBLISHING LTD.
All Rights for MELTED STONE PUBLISHING LTD. in the U.S. and Canada Controlled and Administered by UNIVERSAL - SONGS OF POLYGRAM INTERNATIONAL, INC.
All Rights for EMI MUSIC PUBLISHING LTD. Administered by SONY/ATV MUSIC PUBLISHING LLC, 424 Church Street, Suite 1200, Nashville, TN 37219
All Rights Reserved   Used by Permission

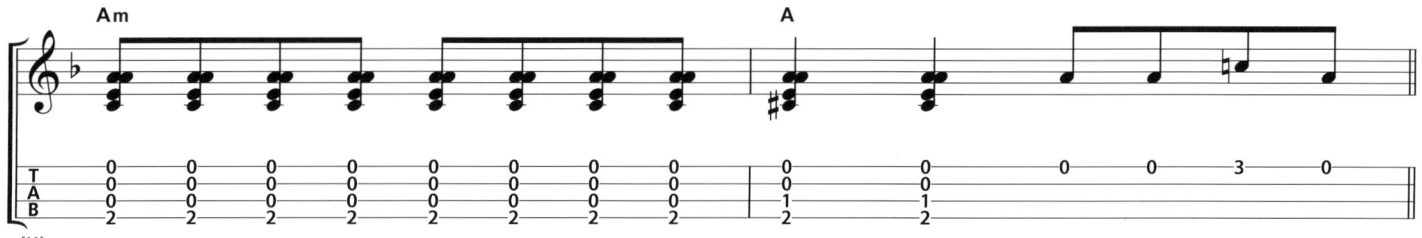
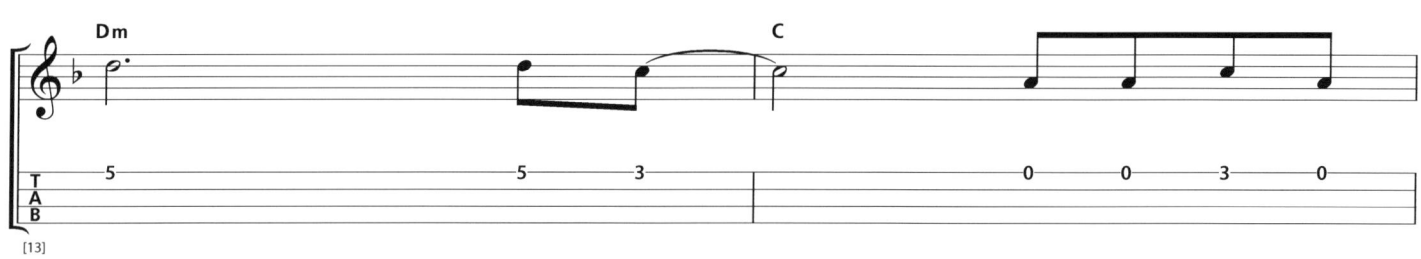
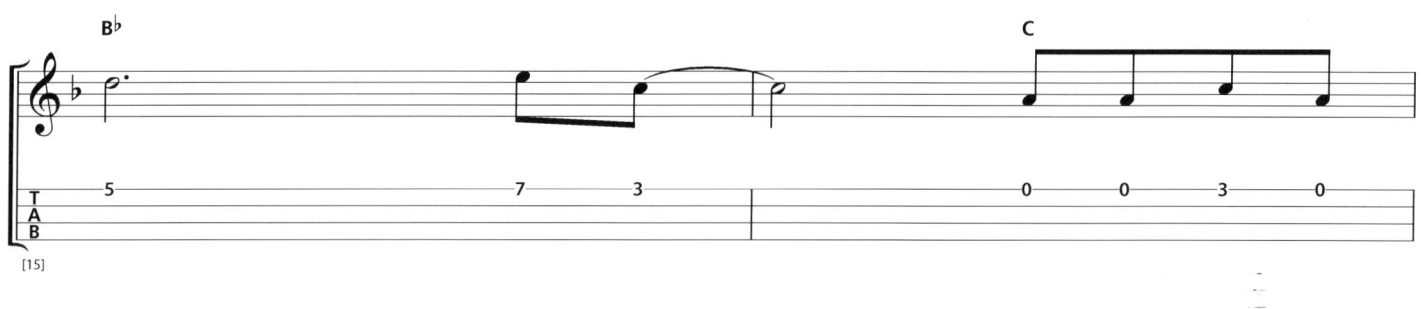
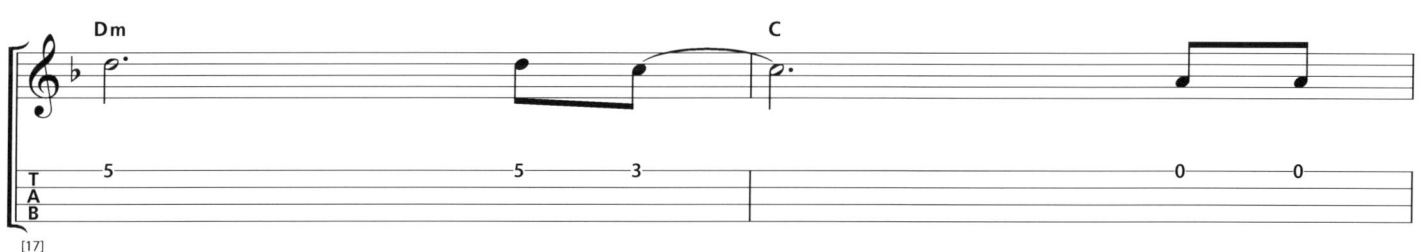
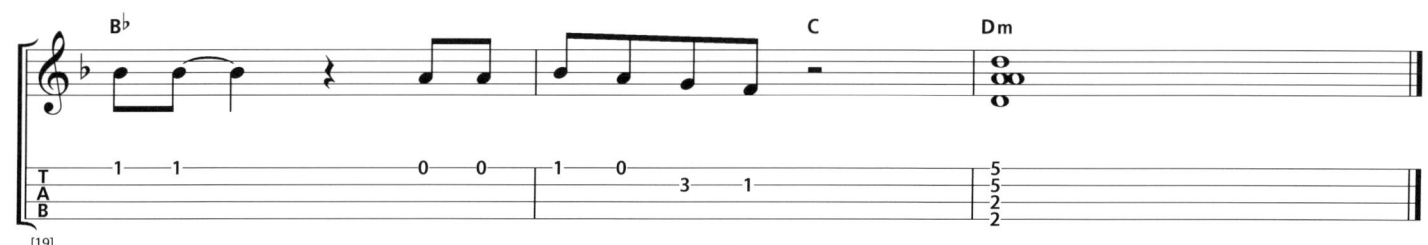

'Shake It Off' | Taylor Swift

Album: *1989*
Label: Big Machine / Republic
Genre: Pop

Chart Peak: 1 (US)
Written By: Taylor Swift, Max Martin, Shellback
Produced By: Max Martin, Shellback

Background Info

'Shake It Off' is one of US recording artist Taylor Swift's many hit-singles, taken from her hugely successful fifth album, *1989* (2014). Written by Swift, Max Martin and Shellback, it is an up-tempo pop track and a noticeable departure from Swift's earlier work that found its roots in popular country music. Martin and Shellback previously worked with Swift on 'We Are Never Ever Getting Back Together'.

'Shake It Off' appears to be dedicated to Swift's detractors as she attempts to strike back at those who have unreasonably pried into her private life. When asked about the topic, she has stated: "I've learned a pretty tough lesson that people can say whatever they want about us at any time, and we cannot control that. The only thing we can control is our reaction to that."

The song premiered during a Yahoo! live stream session on August 18, 2014 (simultaneously streaming internationally online) with its music video, directed by legendary Director Mark Romanek, being released the very same day. Several hours later the song was made available for digital download.

'Shake It Off' became Swift's second number 1 single in the United States. The song won 'Favorite Song' at the 2015 People's Choice Awards and also received nominations for 'Record of the Year', 'Song of the Year' and 'Best Pop Solo Performance' at the 2015 Grammy Awards.

Taylor Swift is one of the most popular recording artists working today. She is known for narrative songs about her personal life, which has seen her receive much media attention since bursting onto the scene. Swift's music contains elements of pop, pop-rock and country. She self-identified as a country artist until the 2014 release of her album *1989*, which she personally describes as a "sonically cohesive pop album".

Since her debut, Swift has released seven studio albums, four of which topped the UK Album Chart. Her accolades include an impressive ten wins at the Grammy Awards and in 2015 she was included in *Rolling Stone's* list of 100 Greatest Songwriters of All Time.

Performance Notes

This is a lively and bright pop song with a fast tempo. You must take care to feel and count the beat when you start learning this song so you stay 'in sync' with the backing track. This is particularly important in the verse because your chords will be in time with the most important words. Play the chords with a crisp, light feel to suit the mood of the song.

You will be playing the same chord sequence throughout. This is a common pop progression, so your audience will feel like they know the song even if they are hearing it for the first time! Practise the chord progression until it feels comfortable, and remember that the G chord lasts for two measures. An interesting feature of this song is the tension in the chord progression. We are playing in the key of G major, but the A minor chord at the start of the progression coupled with the snappy vocals gives the music a sense of urgency and movement.

Look out for the different strumming patterns in each section. Most of the chords only last for one beat, so make sure you feel confident muting the strings in between your strums. You will need to follow the song carefully so you change your strumming pattern as you move into each new section.

Shake It Off

Session Style

Taylor Swift

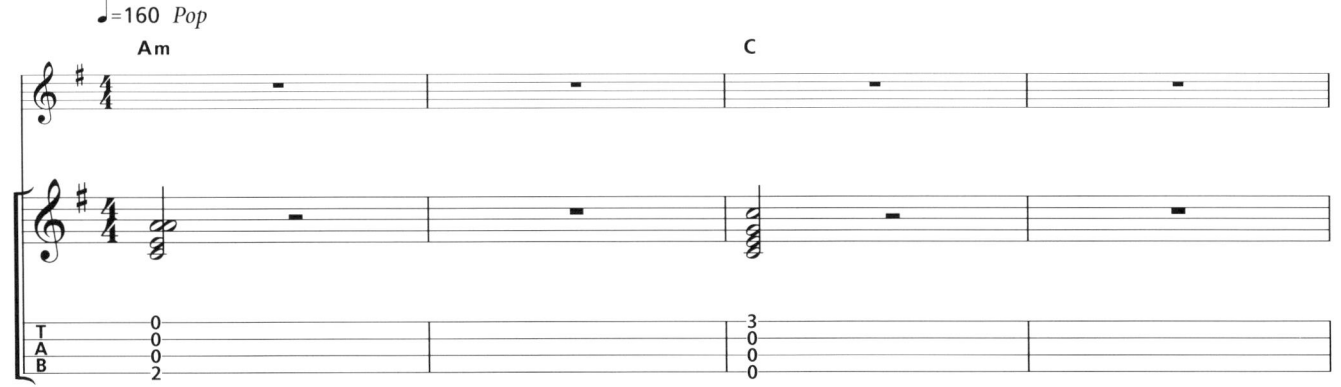
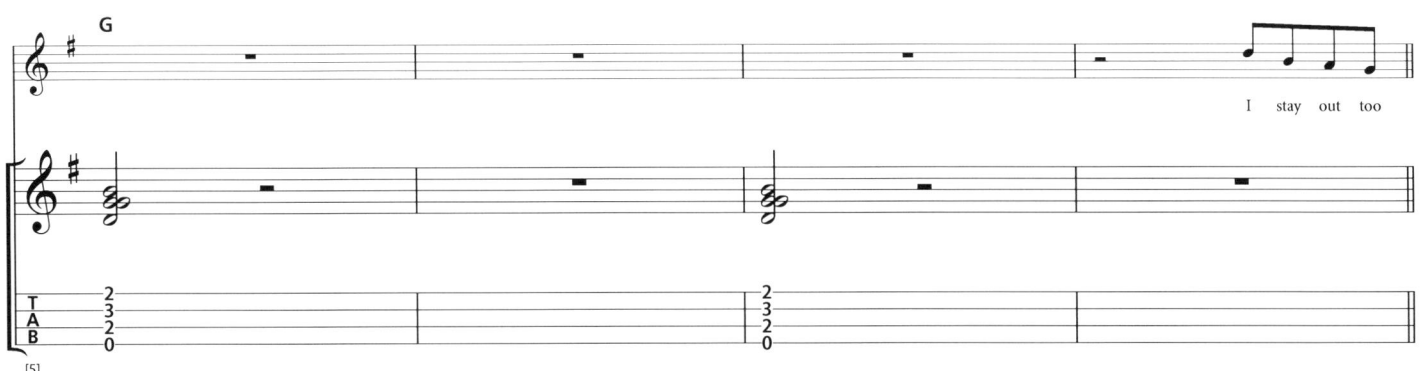
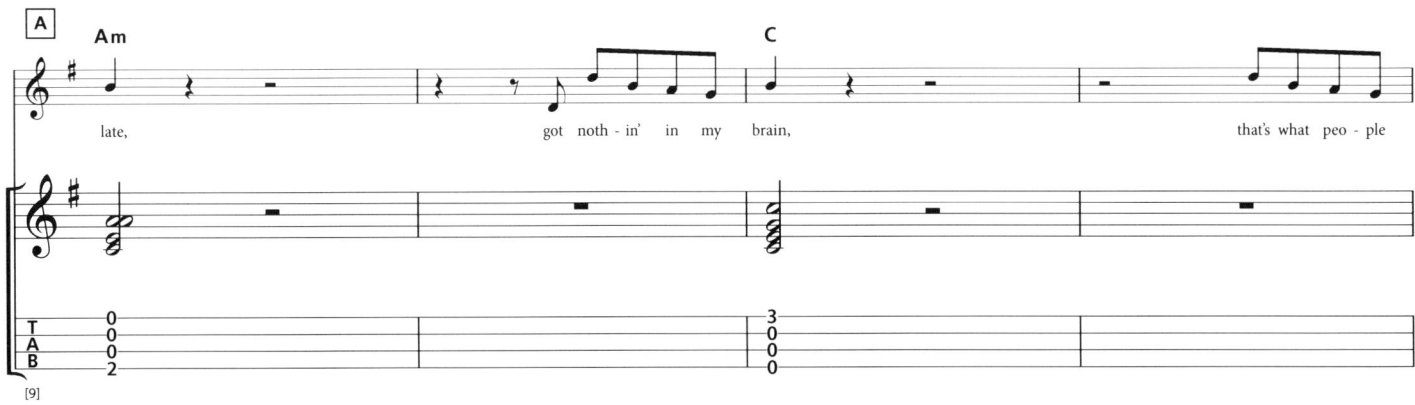

Words and Music by Taylor Swift, Max Martin and Shellback
Copyright © 2014 Sony/ATV Music Publishing LLC, Taylor Swift Music and MXM
All Rights on behalf of Sony/ATV Music Publishing LLC and Taylor Swift Music Administered by Sony/ATV Music Publishing LLC, 424 Church Street, Suite 1200, Nashville, TN 37219
All Rights on behalf of MXM Administered Worldwide by Kobalt Songs Music Publishing
International Copyright Secured   All Rights Reserved

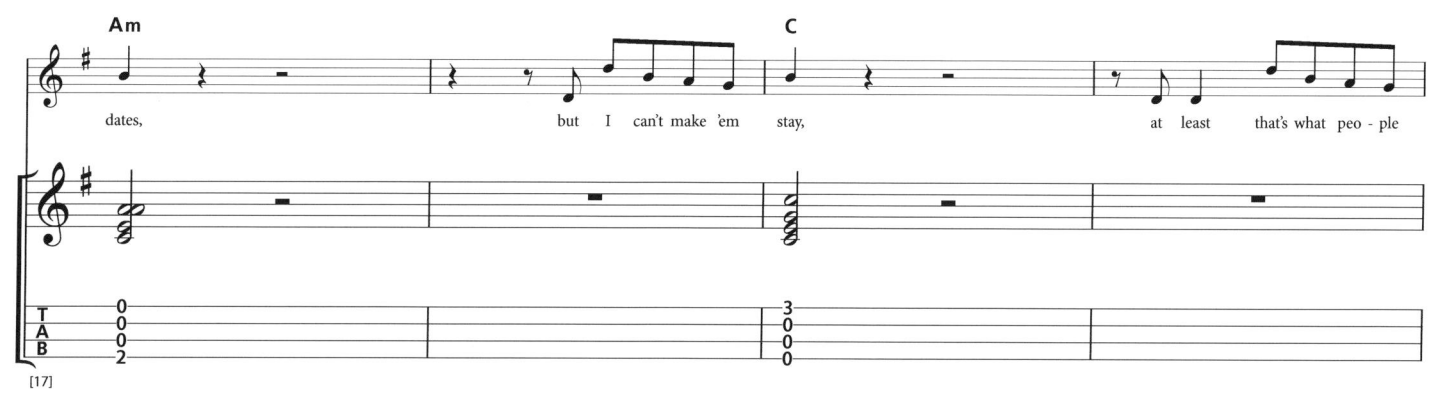

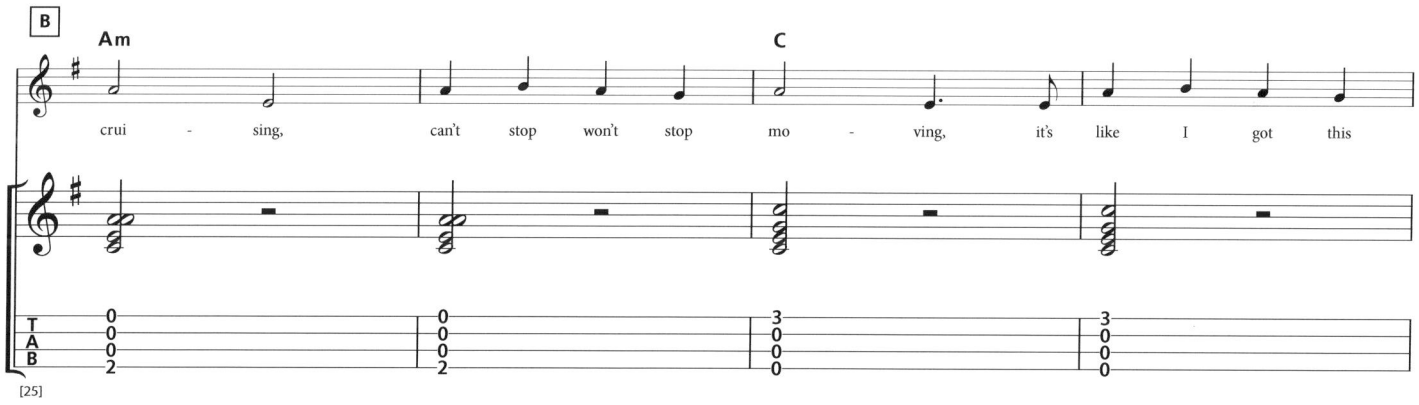
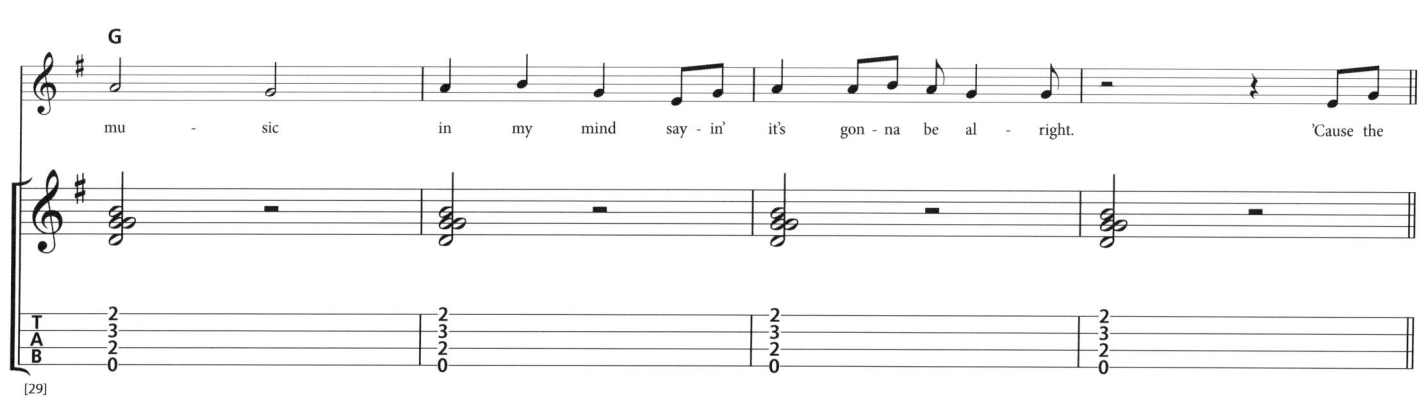

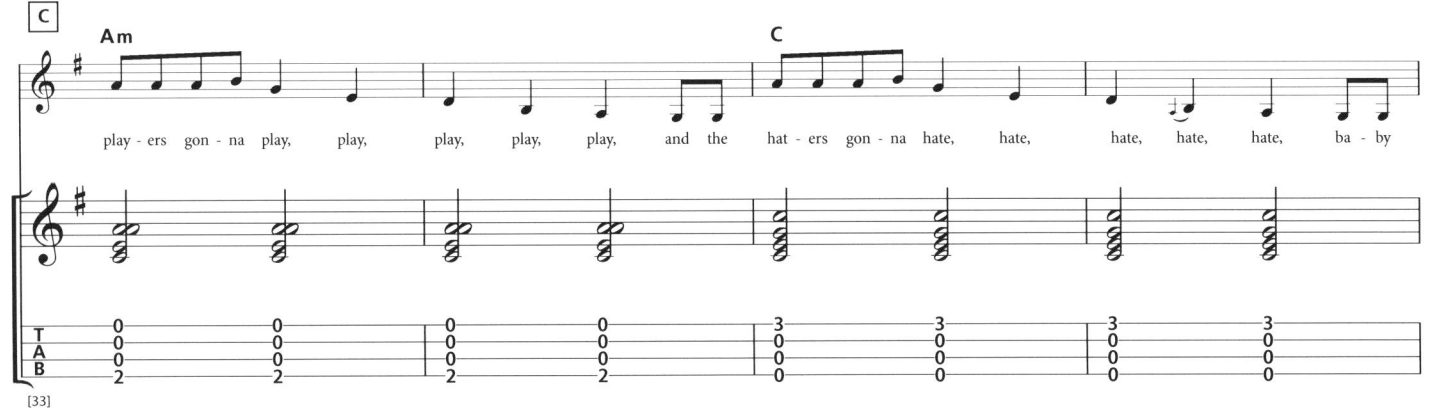
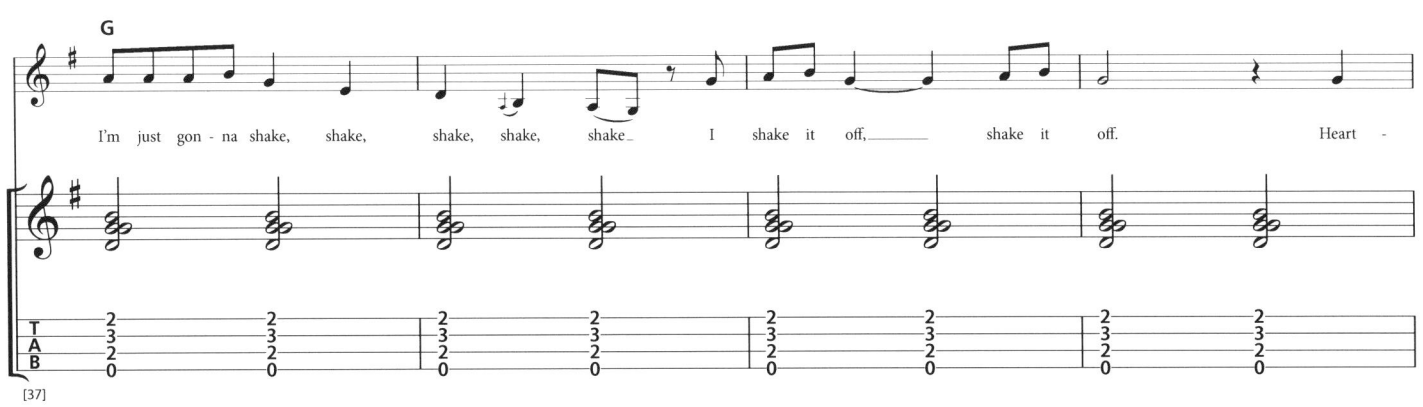
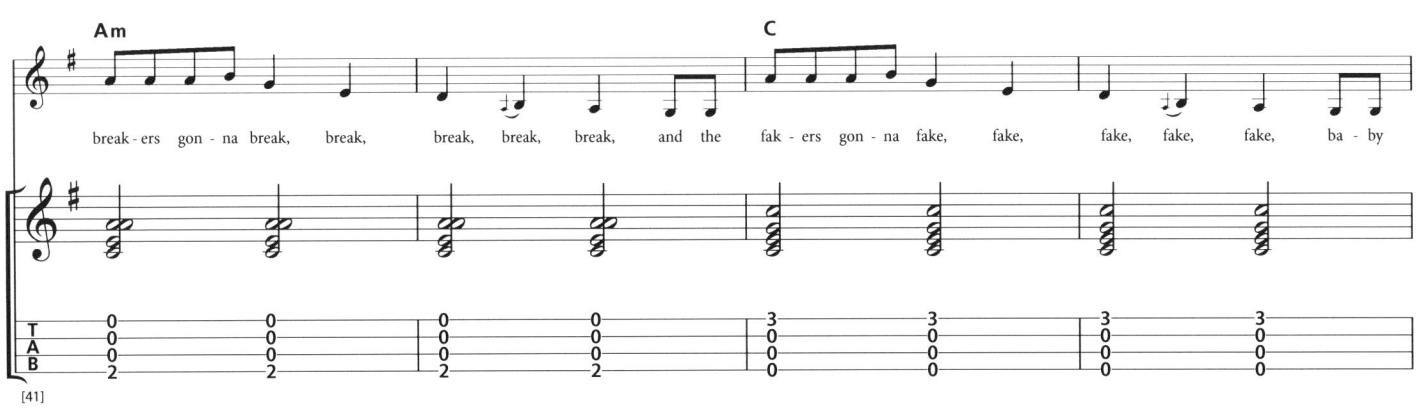
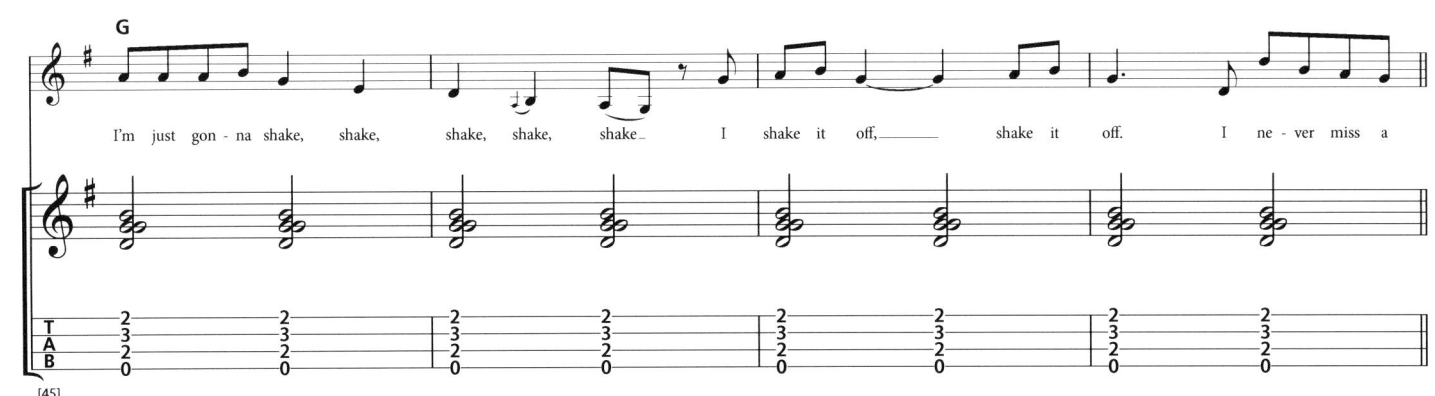

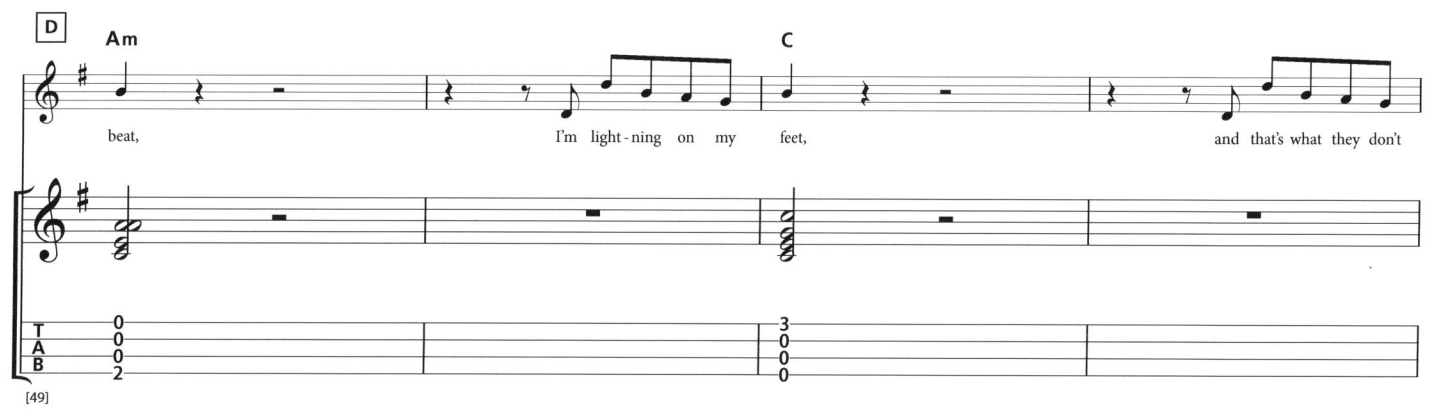

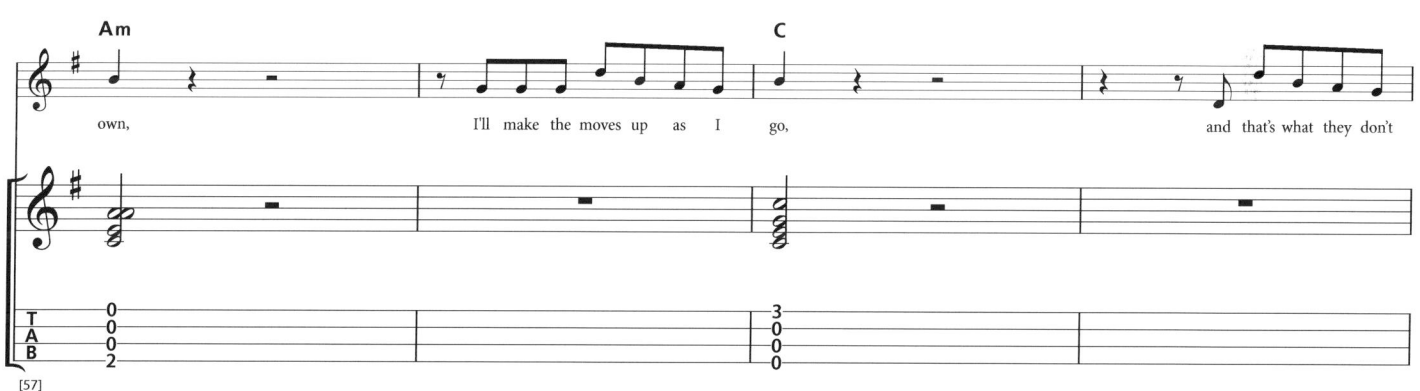

Technical Exercises

At Debut, you will be required to play a selection of exercises drawn from each of the groups below.

All exercises need to be played with a straight feel, using the given rhythmic values at the tempos shown.

Note that Groups A and B need to be played to a click. Group C is played as a sequence with each chord being announced by the assessor.

Group A | Scales
The tempo for this group is ♩=65 bpm.

1. C major scale

2. C major pentatonic scale

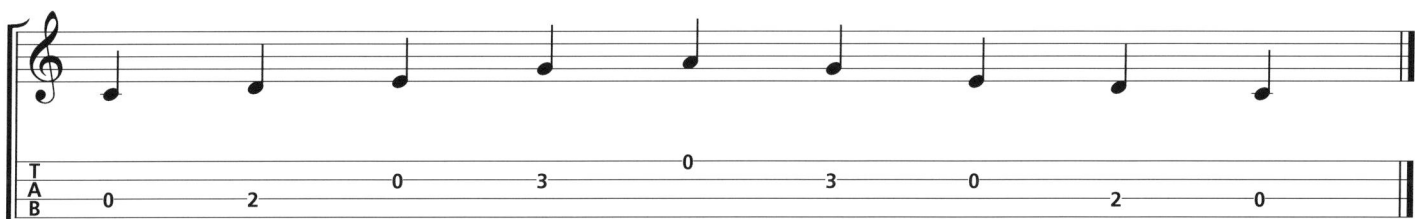

3. A minor pentatonic scale

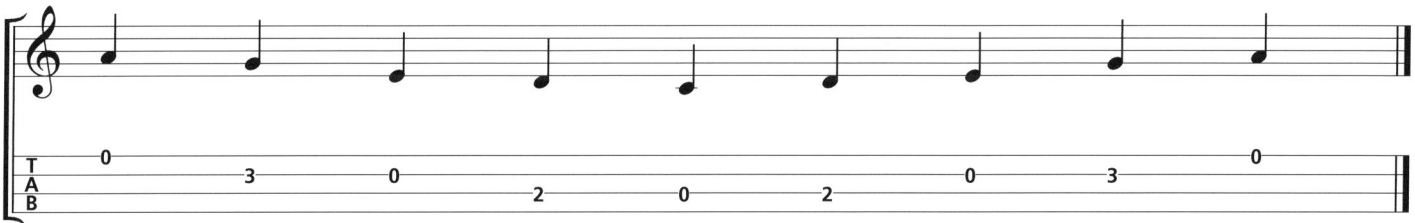

4. G major scale

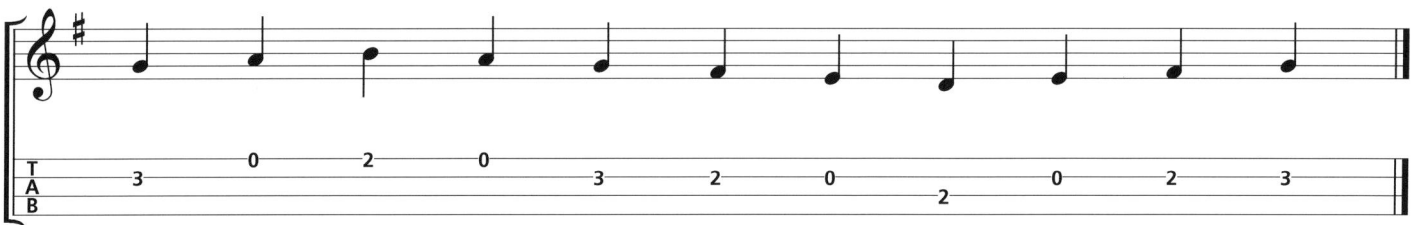

Technical Exercises

Group B | Arpeggios
The tempo for this group is ♩=65 bpm.

1. C major arpeggio

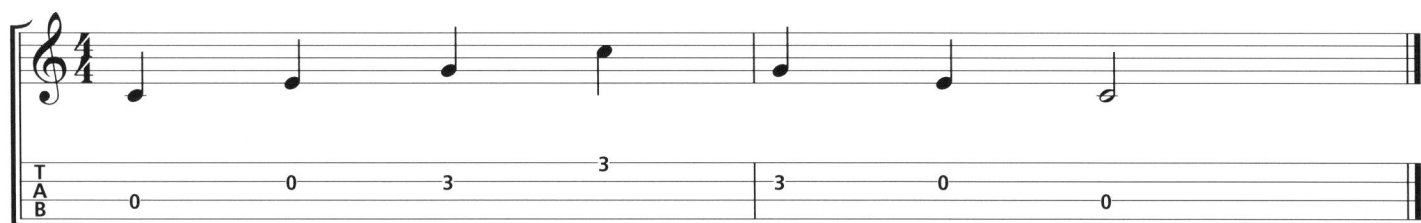

2. A minor arpeggio

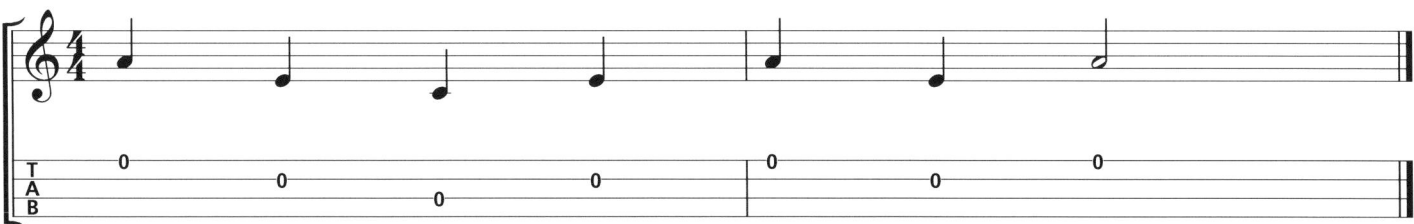

Technical Exercises

Group C | Chord Voicings

Open position chords. Chords to be strummed once as directed by the assessor.

1. Major chords

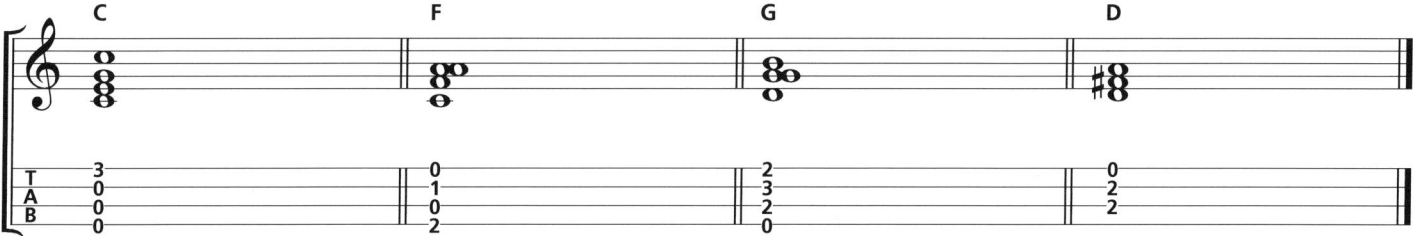

2. Minor chords

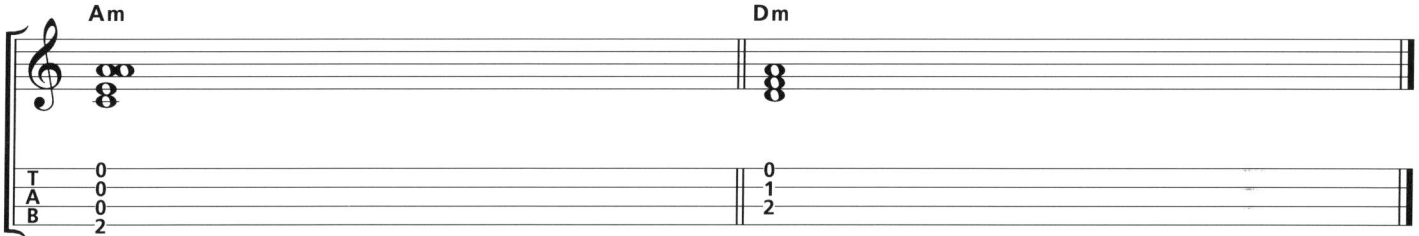

Supporting Tests

Section 1 | Sight Reading

In the assessment, you have a choice between either a Sight Reading test or an Improvisation & Interpretation test within Section 1. The assessor will ask you which one you wish to choose before commencing. Once you have decided, you cannot change your mind.

In the Sight Reading test, the assessor will give you a four measure melody. You will first be given 90 seconds to practise, after which the assessor will play the backing track twice. The first time is for you to practise and the second time is for you to perform the final version for the assessment. For the first playthrough, the backing track will begin with four clicks. For the second playthrough, there will be a one measure count-in. The tempo is ♩=65.

During the practice time, you will be given the choice of a metronome click throughout or a one measure count-in at the beginning. The backing track is continuous, so once the first playthrough has finished, the count-in of the second playing will start immediately.

Tempo: ♩=65
Duration: 4 Measures
Rhythms: Whole notes, half notes and quarter notes
Key: C major
Pitches and Instrumental Compass: C and D on the 3rd string, and E on the 2nd string

Please note: exercises may be performed either fingerstyle or with a plectrum.

Example 1

♩=65

Example 2

♩=65

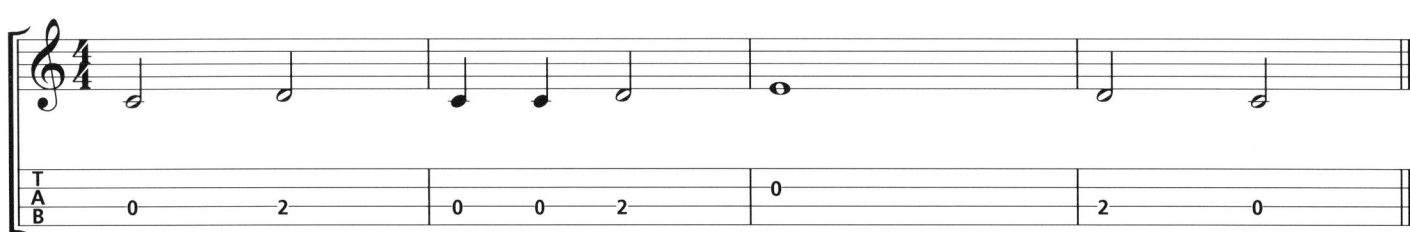

Please note: The tests shown are examples: The assessor will give you a different version in the assessment

Section 1 | Improvisation & Interpretation

In the assessment, you have a choice between either a Sight Reading test or an Improvisation & Interpretation test within Section 1. The assessor will ask you which one you wish to choose before commencing. Once you have decided, you cannot change your mind.

In the Improvisation & Interpretation test, the assessor will give you a four measure chord progression in the key of C major. You will first be given 90 seconds to practise, after which the assessor will play the backing track twice. The first time is for you to practise and the second time is for you to perform the final version for the assessment. For the first playthrough, the backing track will begin with four clicks. For the second playthrough, there will be a one measure count-in. The tempo is ♩=65.

During the practice time, you will be given the choice of a metronome click throughout or a one measure count-in at the beginning.

The backing track is continuous, so once the first playthrough has finished, the count-in of the second playing will start immediately.

At Debut, you only need to improvise single note melodies in the key of C major. The chord symbols show the chord progression of the backing track only.

Example 1

Example 2

Please note: The tests shown are examples: The assessor will give you a different version in the assessment

Supporting Tests

Section 2 | Ear Tests

There are two Ear Tests in this level/grade. The assessor will play each test to you twice. You will find one example of each type of test printed below.

Test 1: Melodic Recall
The assessor will play you two half notes one after the other. You will tell the assessor whether the second note is higher or lower in pitch than the first note. You will hear the test twice.
Each time the test is played it is preceded by a one measure vocal count-in. The tempo is ♩ = 85.

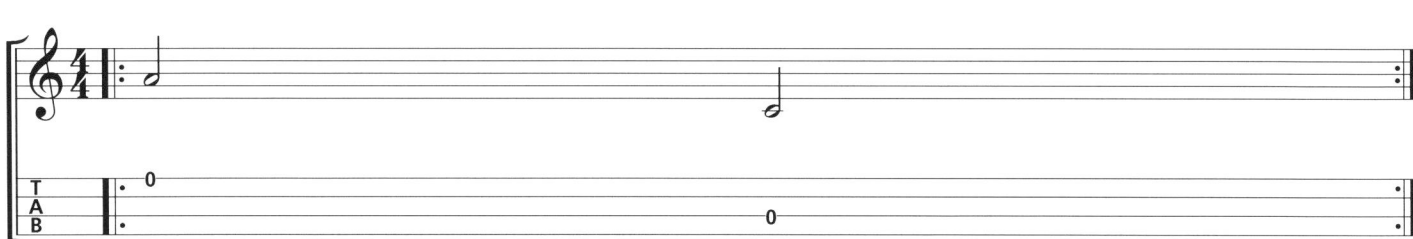

Test 2: Rhythmic Recall
The assessor will play you a two measure rhythm played to a drum backing on the high A string. You will hear the test twice. You will be asked to play the rhythm back. You will then be asked to identify the rhythm from two printed examples shown to you.

Each time the test is played it is preceded by four clicks. There will be a short gap for you to practise. Next you will hear a vocal count-in and you will then play the rhythm to the drum backing. The tempo is ♩ = 85.

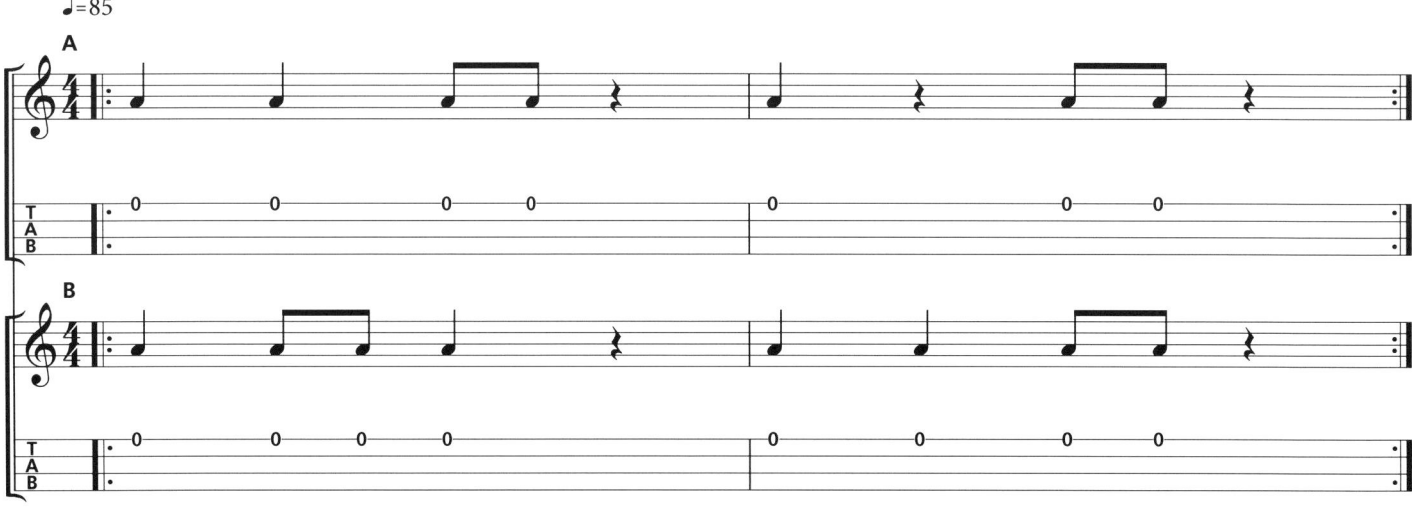

Please note: The test shown is an example: The assessor will give you a different version in the assessment

Supporting Tests

Section 3 | General Musicianship Questions

The final part of your assessment is the General Musicianship Questions section, which features five questions: four relating to one performance piece of your choosing, and the fifth relating to your instrument.

Music Knowledge

The assessor will ask you four music knowledge questions based on a piece of music that you have played in the assessment. You will nominate the piece of music about which the questions will be asked.

In Debut you will be asked to identify:

- The music stave and the TAB
- The treble clef
- Half and quarter note values

Instrument Knowledge

The assessor will also ask you one question regarding your instrument.

In Debut you will be asked to identify:

- One of the following parts of your ukulele: neck, body, tuning-pegs or bridge

About Rockschool Assessments

Entering Rockschool Assessments
Entering a Rockschool assessment is easy, just go online and follow our simple six step process. All details for entering online, dates, fees, regulations and Free Choice Pieces can be found at *www.rslawards.com*

- All candidates should ensure they bring their own Level/Grade syllabus book to the assessment or have proof of digital purchase ready to show the assessor.

Syllabus Guides
You can find further details about Rockschool's Ukulele syllabus by downloading the syllabus guide from our website: *www.rslawards.com*

All candidates should download and read the accompanying syllabus guide when using this level/grade book. Please note that clarifications and updates to syllabus guides are noted at the back of each document.

Performance and Technical Guidance
Students, candidates and teachers may find the following guidance helpful in using the level/grade book and preparing for a Rockschool assessment. Please see below.

- **Tuning**
  Pieces and technical tests have been arranged for re-entrant tuned ukuleles. This is specifically to prepare for the specific techniques which build through the syllabus. If you wish to take a Rockschool assessment using an alternative standard tuning, please contact Rockschool.

- **Fingering**
  Any fingering annotation is given <u>as a guide only</u>. Tablature positions are also given for guidance, except where stipulated to achieve the required technical outcomes (for example, in *campanella* passages).

- **Interpretation**
  Notation should be performed as written, except where there are performance indications to *ad lib. / improvise / develop*, etc. In these instances, the candidate will be marked on their ability to interpret the music in a stylistically appropriate way, commensurate with the level/grade.

- **Adaptation**
  A small degree of adaptation is allowed where, for example, hand stretches do not facilitate the required notated parts. Marks may be deducted if adaptation results in over-simplification of the notation. If in doubt you can submit any adaptation enquiries to: *info@rslawards.com*
  Further adaptation (for example, alternative solos) will be marked according to the equivalent outcomes achieved.

- **Articulation & Dynamics**
  Where articulation and dynamics are marked on the notation, they should be followed. Where it is open to interpretation, the candidate is free to take their own approach, in accordance with the style of the piece.

- **Chord Symbols**
  Most Hit Tune arrangements have chord symbols written above the notation. This is purely for guidance, and to assist the candidate and teacher. Some pieces (for example, film score arrangements) do not contain chord symbol information.

Marking Schemes

DEBUT TO LEVEL/GRADE 5 *

ELEMENT	PASS	MERIT	DISTINCTION
Performance Piece 1	12–14 out of 20	15–17 out of 20	18+ out of 20
Performance Piece 2	12–14 out of 20	15–17 out of 20	18+ out of 20
Performance Piece 3	12–14 out of 20	15–17 out of 20	18+ out of 20
Technical Exercises	9–10 out of 15	11–12 out of 15	13+ out of 15
Sight Reading *or* Improvisation & Interpretation	6 out of 10	7–8 out of 10	9+ out of 10
Ear Tests	6 out of 10	7–8 out of 10	9+ out of 10
General Musicianship Questions	3 out of 5	4 out of 5	5 out of 5
TOTAL MARKS	**60%+**	**74%+**	**90%+**

LEVELS/GRADES 6–8

ELEMENT	PASS	MERIT	DISTINCTION
Performance Piece 1	12–14 out of 20	15–17 out of 20	18+ out of 20
Performance Piece 2	12–14 out of 20	15–17 out of 20	18+ out of 20
Performance Piece 3	12–14 out of 20	15–17 out of 20	18+ out of 20
Technical Exercises	9–10 out of 15	11–12 out of 15	13+ out of 15
Quick Study Piece	6 out of 10	7–8 out of 10	9+ out of 10
Ear Tests	6 out of 10	7–8 out of 10	9+ out of 10
General Musicianship Questions	3 out of 5	4 out of 5	5 out of 5
TOTAL MARKS	**60%+**	**74%+**	**90%+**

PERFORMANCE CERTIFICATES | DEBUT TO LEVEL/GRADE 8 *

ELEMENT	PASS	MERIT	DISTINCTION
Performance Piece 1	12–14 out of 20	15–17 out of 20	18+ out of 20
Performance Piece 2	12–14 out of 20	15–17 out of 20	18+ out of 20
Performance Piece 3	12–14 out of 20	15–17 out of 20	18+ out of 20
Performance Piece 4	12–14 out of 20	15–17 out of 20	18+ out of 20
Performance Piece 5	12–14 out of 20	15–17 out of 20	18+ out of 20
TOTAL MARKS	**60%+**	**75%+**	**90%+**

* Note that there are no Debut Vocal assessments.

Ukulele Notation Explained

THE MUSICAL STAVE shows pitches and rhythms and is divided by lines into measures. Pitches are named after the first seven letters of the alphabet.

TABLATURE graphically represents the ukulele fingerboard. Each horizontal line represents a string, and each number represents a fret.

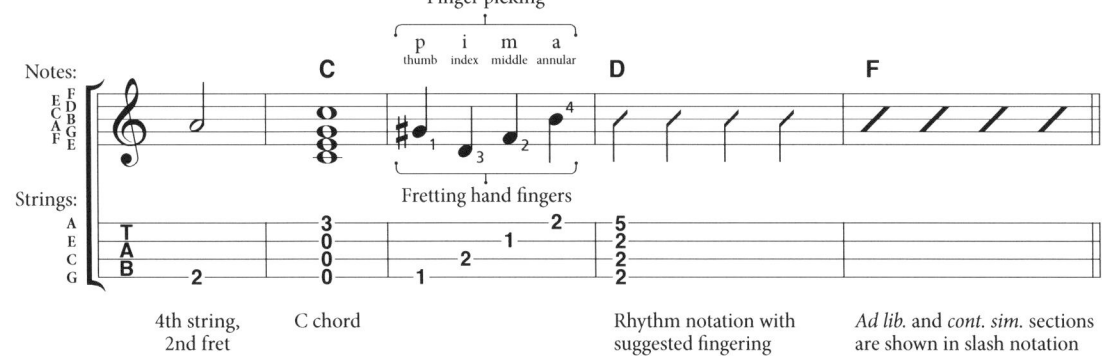

4th string, 2nd fret | C chord | Rhythm notation with suggested fingering | *Ad lib.* and *cont. sim.* sections are shown in slash notation

Definitions For Ukulele Notation

HAMMER-ON: Play the lower note, then sound the higher note by fretting it without repicking.

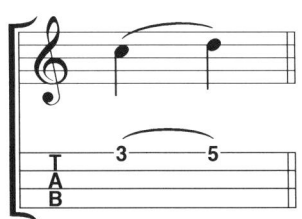

PULL-OFF: Play the higher note then sound the lower note by lifting the finger without repicking.

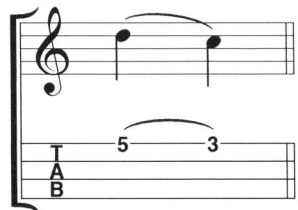

SLIDE: Play the first note, then slide to the next with the same finger.

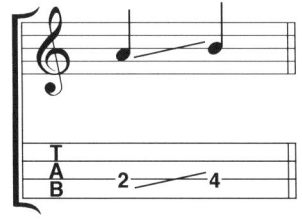

STRING BENDS: Play the first note then bend up or bend down (release the bend) to the pitch indicated in brackets.

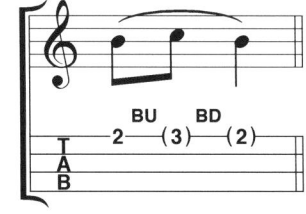

GLISSANDO: A small slide off of a note toward the end of its rhythmic duration. Do not slide 'into' the following note – subsequent notes should be repicked.

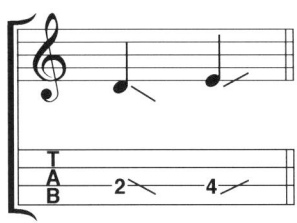

DOWNSTROKE: When using a pick, this symbol indicates a downstroke.

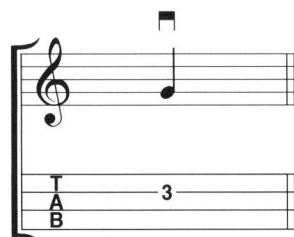

UPSTROKE: When using a pick, this symbol indicates an upstroke.

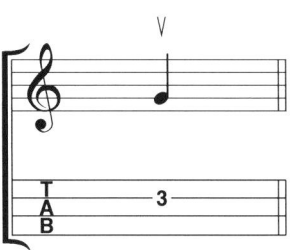

D.%. al Coda
- Go back to the sign (%), then play until the measure marked ***To Coda*** ⊕ then skip to the section marked ⊕ ***Coda***.

D.C. al Fine
- Go back to the beginning of the song and play until the measure marked ***Fine*** (end).

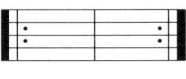
- Repeat the measures between the repeat signs.

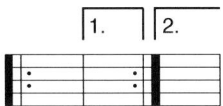
- When a repeated section has different endings, play the first ending only the first time and the second ending only the second time.

Copyright Information

Demons
(Reynolds/McKee/Sermon/Grant/Mosser)
Universal / MCA Music Ltd. / Bluewater Music UK

Knockin' On Heaven's Door
(Dylan)
Sony / ATV Music Publishing (UK) Ltd.

Lean On Me
(Withers)
Universal / MCA Music Ltd.

Marry You
(Mars/Levine/Lawrence)
Warner Chappell North America Ltd. / Universal / MCA Music Ltd. / BMG Rights Management (UK) Ltd.

Rolling In The Deep
(Adkins/Epworth)
EMI Music Publishing Ltd. / Universal Music Publishing Ltd.

Shake It Off
(Swift/Martin/Shellback)
Sony / ATV Music Publishing (UK) Ltd. / Kobalt Music Publishing Ltd.

mcps

rockschool®

DIGITAL DOWNLOADS NOW AVAILABLE!

All your favourite Rockschool titles are now available to download instantly from the RSL shop. Download entire grade books, individual tracks or supporting tests to all your devices.

START DOWNLOADING NOW

www.rslawards.com/shop